NEW DIRECTIONS FOR STUDENT SERVICES

John H. Schuh, *Iowa State University*
EDITOR-IN-CHIEF

Elizabeth J. Whitt, *University of Iowa*
ASSOCIATE EDITOR

Working with Asian American College Students

Marylu K. McEwen
University of Maryland

Corinne Maekawa Kodama
University of Illinois at Chicago

Alvin N. Alvarez
San Francisco State University

Sunny Lee
University of California, Irvine

Christopher T. H. Liang
University of Maryland

EDITORS

Number 97, Spring 2002

JOSSEY-BASS
A Wiley Company
www.josseybass.com

WORKING WITH ASIAN AMERICAN COLLEGE STUDENTS
Marylu K. McEwen, Corinne Maekawa Kodama, Alvin N. Alvarez, Sunny Lee, Christopher T. H. Liang (eds.)
New Directions for Student Services, no. 97
John H. Schuh, Editor-in-Chief
Elizabeth J. Whitt, Associate Editor

Microfilm copies of issues and articles are available in 16mm and 35mm, as well as microfiche in 105mm, through University Microfilms Inc., 300 North Zeeb Road, Ann Arbor, Michigan 48106-1346.

ISSN 0164-7970   ISBN 0-7879-6292-9

NEW DIRECTIONS FOR STUDENT SERVICES is part of The Jossey-Bass Higher and Adult Education Series and is published quarterly by Wiley Subscription Services, Inc., a Wiley company, at Jossey-Bass, 989 Market Street, San Francisco, California 94103-1741. Periodicals postage paid at San Francisco, California, and at additional mailing offices. Postmaster: Send address changes to New Directions for Student Services, Jossey-Bass, 989 Market Street, San Francisco, California 94103-1741.

New Directions for Student Services is indexed in College Student Personnel Abstracts and Contents Pages in Education.

SUBSCRIPTIONS cost $65.00 for individuals and $130.00 for institutions, agencies, and libraries. See ordering information page at end of book.

EDITORIAL CORRESPONDENCE should be sent to the Editor-in-Chief, John H. Schuh, N 243 Lagomarcino Hall, Iowa State University, Ames, Iowa 50011

Cover photograph by Wernher Krutein/PHOTOVAULT © 1990.

Jossey-Bass Web address: www.josseybass.com

Manufactured in the United States of America on acid-free recycled paper containing 100 percent recovered waste paper, of which at least 20 percent is postconsumer waste.

Contents

EDITORS' NOTES

What do you think of when you hear "Asian American students"? Smart, quiet, and industrious—or immigrants, language barriers, and science majors? Or do you realize that you haven't really thought much at all about Asian Americans as a distinct student population? Despite growing numbers of Asian Americans in higher education, the lack of discussion and research specific to Asian Americans has made it difficult to learn about or provide culturally effective services to these students. Currently, the literature on Asian Americans is very specific to a particular research study or functional area and is scattered among various journals and disciplines. As a result, student affairs professionals have not had access to sufficient theory and empirical research to address critical yet basic questions related to Asian American students. For instance, how do race and culture influence Asian American student development? What role does demographic heterogeneity play in the delivery of services to Asian American students? What issues are unique to promoting leadership development and organizational involvement among Asian Americans? What resources are available for student affairs professionals seeking to develop programs, workshops, and training for both student and professional development?

This issue of *New Directions for Student Services* represents a coordinated effort to link the historical, theoretical, and applied literature on Asian American college students into a "one-stop" sourcebook. Rather than focusing on specific functional areas, the content focuses on basic, general information on Asian American college students that should be useful to all practitioners and researchers. This issue is also intended as a stimulus for further discussion among practitioners and researchers about the manner in which student services are designed to meet the needs of Asian Americans in college. Finally, we hope that the ideas in this issue stimulate research on Asian American students, an overlooked population in the literature.

In addressing this group of students, we have chosen to apply the term *Asian American* to a highly diverse population encompassing Americans from East Asian and South Asian backgrounds. Some of the authors have also addressed the concerns of Pacific Islanders, cognizant of the lack of research on Pacific Islanders and the sociopolitical question as to whether they should be grouped in the larger panethnic category of Asian Americans. We believe that the discussions in this issue apply generally to students of Asian descent, but we are less certain that they apply to students of Pacific Island ancestry. We ask that you be conscious of these distinctions as you read this work and as you involve yourself with students of both Asian and Pacific Island descent. We also realize the contradiction in compiling a volume of work about a population about which it is difficult to generalize because of its diversity. However, we believe strongly that the population of Asian American college students demands increased attention and that they share sufficient cultural similarities and common issues to discuss them as a unique student population.

Three undergraduate Asian American students lead off this issue: Sophia, a 1.5-generation Korean American; Angela, a second-generation Pilipina American; and Bao, a first-generation Vietnamese American. They describe their experiences in college, identify some of their supports and challenges, and share their thoughts on how faculty and staff might improve their practices to better reflect the needs of this growing student population.

In Chapter Two, Shirley Hune highlights the diversity of Asian American college students, including population growth patterns, geographical distributions, demographics within colleges and universities, and generational variations. It is crucially important to understand this diversity when working with Asian American students, as these differences affect the ways in which Asian Americans experience college, as well as the kinds of programs and services that would more effectively meet their needs.

In Chapter Three, Bob Suzuki updates his landmark work on the analysis of the model minority myth, a stereotype developed in the 1960s that by imposing great expectations and pressures on Asian Americans continues to plague Asian American students today. He also identifies the stereotype of the "perfidious foreigner," which works in tandem with the model minority myth to generate negative perceptions of Asian Americans. Suzuki discusses how these damaging stereotypes lead to misunderstanding of Asian Americans and a lack of attention to and services for these students in college.

Racial identity theory is the subject of Chapter Four. Most research on racial identity has focused on African Americans, and there is little writing and research on Asian Americans as racial beings. Alvin Alvarez points out the need to consider the racial identity and racial consciousness of Asian American students in order to more fully understand and respond to their experiences, needs, and development in college.

Chapter Five presents an analysis of psychosocial development theory related to Asian American students. Corinne Kodama, Marylu McEwen, Chris Liang, and Sunny Lee find that for Asian Americans, both external and internal forces affect student development, particularly the often opposing influences of Asian and Western values. The authors also propose a new model of Asian American student development that takes these cultural influences into account and in which racial identity plays a central role.

In Chapter Six, Theresa Ling Yeh addresses the issues of Asian Americans who are at educational risk, a rarely discussed subpopulation of the Asian American student community. This lack of discussion is due in part to the pervasiveness of the model minority myth and has resulted in a lack of attention to this growing population, which is perhaps in greatest need of our academic and student services.

In Chapter Seven, Alvin Alvarez and William Liu present a compelling case for the importance of Asian American studies programs and how they can intersect with student affairs to help Asian American students integrate their intellectual growth with their overall psychosocial development. It brings new light to the importance of integration and collaboration between student affairs and academic affairs in facilitating the holistic development of Asian American students.

Chapter Eight presents a discussion of leadership and the ways in which Asian Americans are left out of traditional leadership roles and theories. Chris Liang, Sunny Lee, and Marie Ting discuss reasons for the lack of involvement in traditional leadership roles among Asian American college students and offer strategies for developing socially conscious Asian American student leaders.

In 1987, Charlene Chew-Ogi and Alan Ogi wrote one of the first articles addressing issues of Asian American college students, and it is still cited frequently today. As a result, they were the natural choice to reflect on the topics featured in this issue, addressing the experiences of Asian American college students and suggesting ways for student affairs professionals to respond. The authors also offer questions to encourage thinking on improvement of practice for Asian American college students.

The volume ends with an annotated bibliography of additional sources in which we present selected articles, books, and related resources that we believe are landmark works, comprehensive in scope and greatly relevant to student affairs professionals.

Finally, you may notice that we have five coeditors, unusual in academic publishing. In the spirit of Asian American collectivism, this issue of *New Directions for Student Services* has truly been a collaborative effort from start to finish. This project has come together through three years of dialogue, professional conferences, five-way conference calls, and countless e-mail attachments, along with four job changes, two moves, one pregnancy, and a sabbatical! We would like to thank our chapter authors for their contributions, as well as our numerous colleagues around the country who have provided inspiration and support for this work.

We hope that those of you experienced in working with Asian American students can identify with the topics presented here and find interesting perspectives, explanations, and suggestions to help you in your work. For those of you who are not yet encountering many Asian American students, we hope that this volume will introduce you to issues and perspectives that will help prepare you for the future impact of Asian American students on your campus. We hope that you find this work illuminating, interesting, and useful as we continue to strive for improvement in serving Asian American students at our respective colleges and universities.

Marylu K. McEwen
Corinne Maekawa Kodama
Alvin N. Alvarez
Sunny Lee
Christopher T. H. Liang
Editors

MARYLU K. MCEWEN is associate professor in college student personnel, Department of Counseling and Personnel Services, University of Maryland, College Park.

CORINNE MAEKAWA KODAMA is assistant director, Office of Career Services, University of Illinois at Chicago.

ALVIN N. ALVAREZ is assistant professor and coordinator of the college counseling program, Department of Counseling, San Francisco State University, San Francisco, California.

SUNNY LEE is assistant director, Cross-Cultural Center, University of California, Irvine.

CHRISTOPHER T. H. LIANG is a doctoral student in counseling psychology and instructor in Asian American studies, University of Maryland, College Park.

1

Three college students share their experiences as Asian Americans in college and offer suggestions for improvement in campus programs and services.

Voices of Asian American Students

Angela Lagdameo, Sophia Lee, Bao Nguyen
with Christopher T. H. Liang, Sunny Lee,
Corinne Maekawa Kodama, Marylu K. McEwen

Asian American students will confront issues of their identity; racial, ethnic, and individual identity is learned outside of the classroom. Interestingly enough, this education that students desire attempts to undo some of the subtle oppression that was freely provided to them by elementary, middle, and high schools. The concept of an Asian American identity did not exist in the minds of Asian American high school students due to the lack of text and study on Asian Americans and their contributions to the creation of America. [Bao]

When an undergraduate representative was needed, I went. I sat on committees, review boards, and various meetings while juggling a full course load and a job. In addition, the AASU [Asian American Student Union] was spearheading initiatives that promoted greater awareness of our community. Though I chose to partake in each of these activities, it was a double-edged sword. I soon came to realize that the burden of responsibility, in terms of promoting change, was on the student. [Angela]

Damn this inequality. Damn the stupid people in positions of power who could make at least a penmark of a difference in how the institutional structures could be more conducive to Asian American students' total experience. Damn them for not even caring to ask what they can do to help us. Damn those who ask, who seem concerned, and don't lift a finger to apply what they just heard from us. Damn those whose definition of happy students is so narrow that they don't even consider that our requests are valid just because [they don't] fit into their box of what a happy student should want and need. Who has a say in *our* happiness? Who has the most impact? Who has the positions to make a difference? How would you work with a student like me?

NEW DIRECTIONS FOR STUDENT SERVICES, no. 97, Spring 2002 © Wiley Periodicals, Inc.

What sort of steps would you take to understand my experience on top of the hundreds of other students of color here? [Sophia]

These are the voices of three Asian American college students. In introducing this issue of *New Directions for Student Services,* we wanted to hear directly from today's students about some of their issues, insights, and struggles to remind us of the students who are the motivation for much of our work and to set the context for the following chapters of theory, research, and commentary. We asked Angela, Bao, and Sophia to share their thoughts regarding their experiences in college as Asian American students. We asked them to write freely and honestly, and in selecting excerpts, we have tried to be true to the essence of their original essays.

Their writing illustrates themes of marginalization, inadequate resources and lack of diversity among staff, institutionalized privilege, racism, and the need for a safe space on campus; the students also offer suggestions and insights to higher education professionals. In reading their thoughts, consider how these students' concerns may be similar to or different from those of the Asian American students on your campus.

Feeling Marginalized, Misunderstood, and Disconnected from the College Campus

One of my professors told me that Asian American students are apathetic and they are here just to study and get their degree and get out. Students are disconnected due to the fact that they cannot relate to the people who are making the decisions that affect them. It is difficult for students to accept and take ownership of an institution when they feel that they are not a part of the institution. The university needs to change its routine and enact creative methods to recruit quality Asian American administrators—chancellors, vice chancellors, and directors. The university lacks the diversity in leadership that has manifested itself to a campus that too many say lacks spirit and pride. [Bao]

Countless students of color are still accepting that less than equal and best treatments are commonplace occurrences in school. There is no system of appeals or checks to realize the unfair experiences for the students of color compared to their white counterparts. There just doesn't seem to be any room in the large agenda of the student affairs practitioners to try to accommodate *all* of the student population. So devastating experiences continue to happen to students of color. [Sophia]

As a junior, I do not feel foolish to ask where the adequate resources for APAs [Asian Pacific Americans] are. I continue to search for outreach from the administration, faculty, and staff. However, the APA community has just begun to be understood; misconceptions still plague the APA community. I want to arrive at the point where freshmen feel welcomed and understood when they enter any office on campus or are greeted by any staff member. I want to be assured that each faculty member or administrator is well versed on the issues pertaining to APAs even before APAs address them. [Angela]

Inadequate Resources and Diversity Among Staff

Many students go about college without having a role model to be able to acknowledge that they are capable of achieving high goals. The university campus is visibly diverse among the student population, yet the leadership in administration does not reflect the demographics of the students. This is an important issue that needs to be addressed when there is only one Asian American administrator for a campus that is almost 60 percent Asian American. The result of the lack of a diverse administration leads these students to [feel] detached from the university. [Bao]

In terms of adequate support, there was only one part-time graduate student whose job description was specific to working with the APA population. I quickly learned that I had to operate under a limited budget and limited personal resources. If I needed to talk to someone who would understand me entirely—culturally and personally—other than my peers, who would I turn to? I was aware of the many faculty, staff, and administrative positions and offices that were offering their facilities and time, yet they were not as well versed on APA issues. I now realize how essential it is for APAs to be able to relate to someone of the same or similar cultural background. It is key for APAs to have the option of learning from someone who has personal experience coupled with book knowledge to make sense of and to validate what they are feeling. [Angela]

While my organization of concerned students continued to arrange meetings and stressfully prepare an argument to ask the administration to take action, these boys practiced their skits that were homophobic, sexist, and just stupid. While our organization struggled to prove that students in power were racist enough to slash our budget by 84 percent, these boys used their funds to print offensive flyers depicting racially stereotypical images. [Sophia]

Institutionalized Privilege and Racism

I realized that institutionalized privilege, exemplified by a number of offices and staff, was rampant among historically white organizations. This is one structural example in which the ideological expression of privilege covertly haunts APAs and other communities. I feel that staff members and directors of prominent offices on campus need to be more acutely aware of the structures of their respective offices. In a prominent office on campus, there are three full-time staff members to work with the Greek community, versus only one part-time graduate student each assigned to work with the APA, lesbian, gay, bisexual, transgender, Latino, and black communities. [Angela]

How can student leaders correctly voice the opinions of Asian American students if all the leaders are white students? . . . I raise two very basic questions: (1) How are students ever going to understand the differences in experiences between Asian Americans and others if even the negative and threatening issues are not allowed to be raised? (2) Why are student affairs practitioners not working to overcome [the] obvious disregard for so many of their students of color's needs? You cannot possibly sell the diversity of the school to outsiders and comment about how wonderful programs and life on campus are if there is still discrimination. That sends a message to the students of color that they are not worth as much as the white students are. And that their voices are not to be heard because other students, white students, can speak for them and everything will be fine. [Sophia]

Having a Safe Space on Campus

I immediately found comfort in the Asian American Student Union. The AASU enabled me to be more aware of my identity as an Asian Pacific American woman and allowed me to foster my culture in a safe space. [Angela]

The most valuable asset that the university possesses is its cross-cultural center—its staff, leadership and opportunities for leadership development, physical space, and friendly atmosphere. The center gives students a physical space to celebrate their diversity. It provides leadership through qualified leaders who also happen to reflect more of the demographics of the student population. Students are then able to organize, be creative, and—most important—learn. The cross-cultural center offers students a comfortable environment to obtain everything needed that is missing in the classroom and lecture halls. [Bao]

The Asian American mentor program is a student-run organization to help first-year students transition into college life and also provide workshops to educate students on APA issues. After I went through training week as a mentor, the world changed tints and shades. I saw it in a different light, from a different perspective, and with a thirst to understand more of the societal structures we live in. I realized that I had a much bigger desire to achieve things not only for myself but also for my community on campus. I saw all these possibilities for just a small population of Asian American students on campus, and the thought of extending that sort of work beyond the college "bubble" was astounding to me. [Sophia]

Suggestions for Higher Education Professionals

I implore staff members to be more critical of the implications that come with every program that they advocate for. At a college level, it is imperative for staff to be responsible for deconstructing stereotypes that are rampant among our communities. For Asian American students, who are perceived as the "silent, model minority," it is extremely important to avoid programs that foster these stereotypes. [Angela]

This community can learn from itself and turn around to teach others, but it must be given the room to grow. Students [obtaining] firsthand experience in this is key to their growth in their ethnic and social identity. Student affairs practitioners, faculty, and administration should embrace these sorts of programs and use their positions to support and encourage growth in this area. [Sophia]

I recall wishing that the bulk of the outreach from faculty, staff, and administrators was more proactive than reactive; I wanted to witness them actively engaging with the APA community. I believe that it is necessary for the administrators to use their positions to create purposeful programs that would enhance the campus climate. . . . . It is disheartening to attend "diversity" initiatives and a plethora of other similar committees when those who called for the meeting are not present; the administration is represented by graduate students. In addition, there are rarely public reports on the results of these initiatives. Thus students who have exhausted their efforts and compromised their class schedules to participate feel shortchanged. [Angela]

Angela's, Bao's, and Sophia's are messages strong, insightful, and meaningful. They offer powerful imperatives to us in higher education not only to take notice of what they say but also, even more important, to hold ourselves and our profession accountable to developing practices, policies, and theories that promote the education and development of Asian American students. As you read the other chapters of this issue, we ask you to keep in mind these students' thoughts, concerns, and passions and to consider what their messages mean for you in *your* work with Asian American college students.

ANGELA LAGDAMEO *is a second-generation Pilipina American attending a large public research university on the East Coast.*

SOPHIA LEE *is a "1.5-generation" Korean American attending a small, private liberal arts college in California.*

BAO NGUYEN *is a first-generation Vietnamese American attending a midsized public research university in California.*

CHRISTOPHER T. H. LIANG *is a doctoral student in counseling psychology and instructor in Asian American studies, University of Maryland, College Park.*

SUNNY LEE *is assistant director, Cross-Cultural Center, University of California, Irvine.*

CORINNE MAEKAWA KODAMA is assistant director, *Office of Career Services, University of Illinois at Chicago.*

MARYLU K. MCEWEN is associate professor in college student personnel, *Department of Counseling and Personnel Services, University of Maryland, College Park.*

2

The author provides an overview of the Asian American population, its immigration patterns and trends, current demographics, and higher educational statistics and explains why student affairs professionals need to address the diversity of Asian American students if they are to be better served and supported.

Demographics and Diversity of Asian American College Students

Shirley Hune

The Asian American population is one of the fastest-growing racial groups in the United States and in higher education. As a racial category, it is not fixed but a fluid umbrella grouping that has evolved over the past three decades out of "dynamic and complex negotiations between state interests, panethnic demands, and ethnic-specific challenges" (Espiritu and Omi, 2000, p. 43).

The term *Asian American* originated during the social reform efforts of the late 1960s to end racial discrimination. College activists of different Asian ethnicities adopted it as a panethnic identity to acknowledge their similar treatment as minority group members and as a strategy to form political coalitions for equity and empowerment (Wei, 1993). In the 1970s, the U.S. Census Bureau sought to gather statistics on ethnic groups that government officials deemed similar and created the "Asian or Pacific Islander" (API) category. After Asian and Pacific groups protested the loss of their distinctiveness by this action, the Census Bureau retained separate data collection on ethnic-specific groups in conjunction with a summary API category. At different times, various ethnic-specific groups, including Asian Indians, Pilipinos, and Native Hawaiians, have sought inclusion in or exclusion from the API category because they disagree with it. Such efforts to dispute or expand this racial category to better meet their self-definition and interests will no doubt continue and underscores the complexity of the Asian American population (Espiritu and Omi, 2000).

The author thanks Jo Anne Beazley and Kenyon S. Chan for their data analysis and editorial assistance.

Building panethnic coalitions and developing a panethnic identity have been challenging for Asian Americans, especially with the arrival of new groups and differing ethnic-specific group interests (Espiritu, 1992). Nonetheless, *Asian American* (or *Asian Pacific American* or *Asian and Pacific Islander*) is now a term in common use in institutional data and U.S. society. Most important, it has come to represent numerous groupings as if they are a single coherent category.

This chapter provides an overview of the Asian American population, its immigration patterns and trends, current demographics, and higher education statistics and calls attention to its *heterogeneity*. In this chapter, the term *Asian American* and the data include Pacific Islanders. Asian Americans share commonalities, but they also have differences in such areas as income, ethnicity, culture, and political leanings. The tendency in public policies to exclude Asian Americans or to oversubscribe to their being homogeneous is a disservice to them. For example, Asian American students are both highly visible and invisible on U.S. campuses. They are highly visible in their record numbers and when touted as a "model minority." At the same time, they often are invisible in campus policies and programs (Hune, 1998). This chapter seeks to better inform professionals in higher education about the demographics and diversity of Asian Americans whose interests and issues vary widely and are underserved. An understanding of the complexity of this population is important in developing policies, programs, and services that are more responsive to the needs of Asian American college students.

Immigration Patterns and Trends

Contemporary Asian Americans consist of individuals and descendants of individuals who arrived in the United States first in a trickle and then in two large waves of immigration. Little is known of the early Asian American settlers of the eighteenth century, prior to what is considered the "first wave." They included Pilipino seamen who left the Spanish galleon trade and formed communities in southeastern Louisiana in the mid-1760s and Asian Indians who arrived on English and American vessels in the 1790s as part of the India trade and served as household servants of sea captains in Massachusetts or fared worse as indentured servants or slaves in Pennsylvania (Okihiro, 1994).

Longtime Asian Americans are descendants of the first wave of Asian migration to the U.S. mainland and Hawaii of the second half of the nineteenth century and the early twentieth century. Nearly one million Asian men and women helped develop the western states. The vast majority of the 370,000 Chinese (1840s to 1880s), 400,000 Japanese (1880s to 1920), and 180,000 Pilipinos, 7,000 Koreans, and 7,000 Asian Indians (1900s to 1930) were laborers (Chan, 1991). Some became small business operators. Their lives were constrained by racial discrimination, economic exploitation, limited political and civil rights, and immigration restrictions that curtailed family reunification. During World War II, the second generation, that is, children of the first wave, raised war bonds, joined the armed forces, or were confined to internment camps (Chan, 1991). The third generation was part of the 1960s and 1970s college population that sought to transform higher education with demands for access and equity in admissions, ethnic studies programs, and the hiring of more minority faculty (Wei, 1993).

Most Asian Americans today, however, are part of the second migration wave, whose experiences in Asia and the United States are distinct from the Americans born of the first wave. Recent immigrants, notably large numbers of Chinese, Pilipinos, Koreans, and Asian Indians, gained entry after the 1965 Immigration Act. That act and subsequent others ended Asian immigration restrictions of the earlier period, promoted family reunification, and gave preferences to professionals in fields in short supply in the United States (scientists, doctors, nurses, high-tech specialists) and to unskilled workers willing to take jobs shunned by domestic American workers (garment workers, small retailers).

New Asian Americans are also refugees, an outcome of U.S. military involvement in Southeast Asia. Nearly one million Vietnamese, Cambodians, and Laotians immigrated under the 1975 Indochina Migration and Refugee Assistance Act, the 1980 Refugee Act, and the 1987 Amerasian Homecoming Act. Some had privileged backgrounds or social networks to facilitate their adjustment, but most arrived impoverished and have had to rebuild lives torn apart by war, dislocation, and trauma (Chan, 1991). Recent arrivals benefited from an improved civil rights environment and new economic and political opportunities, including the elimination of legal forms of racial discrimination and affirmative action policies, which have since been eroded. Although overt forms of racism have diminished, subtle forms persist, and Asian Americans continue to be victims of racial violence and hate crimes (Umemoto, 2000).

The post-1965 arrivals have dramatically changed U.S. and Asian American demographics. The Asian American population has grown from 1.5 million in 1970 to 3.7 million in 1980 to 7.3 million in 1990 (U.S. Census Bureau, 1993b). In June 2000, it was estimated at 11.1 million, or 4 percent of the U.S. population (U.S. Census Bureau, 2000). Longtime Asian American communities have also been transformed. New Asian Americans are more heterogeneous, representing a vast array of homelands, class backgrounds, languages, and religions. The Asia Pacific region is now a primary source of U.S. immigration, providing about one-third of the nation's annual quota. While the sending states bemoan the "brain drain" and loss of labor power, the United States as a receiving state is a beneficiary. If the nation's need for professionals and unskilled workers persists, as is highly likely, the Asian American population will continue to increase and diversify through new immigration in the twenty-first century. In short, Asian Americans are an integral part of the economic, cultural, and political life of the nation, including its colleges and universities.

Current Demographic Data

An analysis of data on Asian Americans from the 1990 census (the most thorough assessment until 2000 census data are available) uncovers important differences *among* and *within* the many ethnic groups that make up the population.

National and Ethnic Diversity. In 1990, Asian Americans accounted for 3 percent of the nation's population, but within the umbrella API category, the census identified fifty-seven groups, attesting to its heterogeneity. Six groups comprised the vast majority: the Chinese (22.6 percent of all APIs), Pilipinos (19.3 percent), Japanese (11.7 percent), Asian Indians (11.2 percent), Koreans (11.0 percent), and Vietnamese (8.4 percent). Smaller groups include Native Hawaiians, Hmong, Laotians, Thais, Samoans, Guamanians, Burmese, Sri Lankans, Malayans, Indonesians, Pakistanis, Bangladeshis, Tongans, Fijians, Palauians, and Tahitians (U.S. Census Bureau, 1993b).

There is diversity within groups as well. For example, Asians from India differ in religion, language, and social background as well as in generation in the United States. To add to the complexity, many Asian Americans are multiracial. They are often misrepresented in the census, in higher education, and elsewhere and find that their issues are ignored (Espiritu and Omi, 2000).

Native-Born Versus Foreign-Born. Recent arrivals have shifted Asian Americans from a native-born to a predominantly foreign-born population. In 1990, some 63.1 percent were born in a country other than the United States, compared with 36 percent of Hispanics and 3.3 percent of whites (U.S. Census Bureau, 1993a). Foreign-born status differs across Asian American groups. For example, Japanese Americans are primarily U.S.-born, while Vietnamese, Laotian, Cambodian, and Hmong Americans are largely foreign-born, reflecting their post-1975 refugee status (Hune and Chan, 1997).

Language Diversity and Proficiency. Asian Americans are diverse in native language and English language ability. English is generally the first and often the only language of the American-born. In contrast, most foreign-born Asian Americans speak a language other than English. Many are fluently bilingual and even multilingual or speak more than one dialect of their native Asian language. Those with limited English proficiency generally live in households where a language other than English predominates (Hune and Chan, 1997).

Geographical Location and Housing Characteristics. Asian Americans are both highly concentrated in cities and one region of the United States and geographically dispersed across the nation. In 1990, they resided in every state, but nearly 58 percent of them lived in the West, home to only 21 percent of the U.S. population as a whole. Nearly 70 percent were in six states: California, Hawaii, Illinois, New York, Texas, and Washington.

Asian Americans are highly urbanized, more than any other racial or ethnic group, and that adds to their household expenses. In metropolitan areas, Asian American families were far more likely than whites (24 percent versus 3 percent) to live in crowded conditions (Hune and Chan, 1997).

Family Characteristics. In 1990, Asian American families were generally headed by married couples (82 percent), much like all U.S. families (79.5 percent). Their average family size (3.74 persons) was smaller than that of Hispanic families (3.84 persons) but greater than that of white families (3.06 persons), black families (3.46 persons), and American Indian families (3.57 persons). Asian American family size also varied, ranging from 6.4 persons for Hmong Americans to 3.1 persons for Japanese Americans (U.S. Census Bureau, 1993a).

Income and Poverty. National data and notions of a racial minority "success story" should be viewed cautiously. Asian American median family income was the highest ($46,637) among all racial and ethnic groups in 1998, yet per capita income for Asian Americans ($18,709) was lower than the per capita income of white households ($22,952) (U.S. Census Bureau, 1999). The number of wage earners per family and their location help explain this. In part, due to their lower per capita income than whites and their need for mutual support, Asian Americans had the highest percentage of three or more wage earners per family among all racial and ethnic groups in 1990. They also were concentrated in high-income, high-cost urbanized areas (Hune and Chan, 1997).

Aggregated per capita income can hide differences among Asian American groups. Disaggregated data are available in the 1990 census but not in current statistics. They reveal that Japanese, Asian Indian, and Chinese Americans, many of whom are professionals, earned more than the national per capita average of $14,420, but other Asian Americans, including all Southeast Asian and Pacific Islander groups, earned significantly less, with a low of $2,692 per capita income for Hmong Americans. Although the poverty rates for Asian American groups are much lower than for African Americans, Hispanics, and American Indians, they are nearly double the rates for whites. Therefore, certain Asian American groups are at economic risk (Hune and Chan, 1997).

Labor Participation and Occupational Characteristics. Asian Americans have a higher rate of labor participation than the overall U.S. population (U.S. Census Bureau, 1993b). In 1990 census occupational data, Asian American employment in technical sales and administrative support (33 percent) and service (14.6 percent) was similar to all Americans (32 and 13.2 percent). More Asian Americans (31.2 percent) were in the managerial and professional specialty than all Americans (26 percent). However, gross census occupational categories do not adequately measure status, work conditions, opportunities, or lack of them. For example, some Asian Americans brought capital and professional expertise to the United States and do manage other workers. Other Asian American professionals have reached middle management in the public or private sphere, but many report a glass ceiling blocking their advancement. Still others are called "managers" but work in small family businesses with low returns and long hours and often at risk of physical harm. Participation in various occupational categories also differs by ethnicity. For example, 43.6 percent of Asian Indians were managers or professionals, compared with 5 percent of Laotians. These disparities reflect differences in education and skills of recent arrivals (Hune and Chan, 1997; Woo, 1994).

Educational Data, Trends, and Issues

Asian American educational attainment is generally high, but national data are misleading. In the western region only, where the Asian American population is concentrated, educational attainment is less than that of whites in some respects. It is also bimodal; some Asian Americans have many years of schooling, and others have very little. In 1990, of persons twenty-five years old and over in the West, 10.8 percent of Asian Americans had an eighth-grade education or less, 83.9 percent had a high school diploma or more, and 34.7 percent had a bachelor's degree or more, compared to 3.1, 90.3, and 28.1 percent for whites, respectively. Asian American women had less education than their male counterparts but completed college at a higher rate (32.5 percent) than white women (23.8 percent) (Hune and Chan, 1997).

In part, this complexity reflects the varied educational and occupational background of post-1965 immigrants and refugees. High educational attainment, whether earned in the United States or abroad, has not resulted in Asian American income parity with whites, however. In 1993, the median annual earnings of full-time workers twenty-five years of age and older with a bachelor's degree or more were $36,844 for Asian Americans, compared to $41,094 for whites and $40,240 for all Americans (Hune and Chan, 1997).

The high participation rate of Asian Americans in higher education reflects their demographic trends and high school achievements. Although high school achievement is uneven across Asian American groups and within each group, many more Asian American youth than those of other racial and ethnic groups expect to attend and complete college. They also spend more hours studying and take more academic courses in high school than other racial and ethnic groups, and this enhances their college eligibility. In 1990, the Asian American college enrollment rate was 55.1 percent, compared to 34.4 percent for all Americans aged eighteen to twenty-four years. However, it differs widely within the Asian American population, from 66.5 percent for Chinese Americans and 63.5 percent for Japanese Americans to 28.9 percent and 26.3 percent for Native Hawaiians and Laotian Americans, respectively (Hune and Chan, 1997; U.S. Census Bureau, 1993a).

Current Higher Education Enrollment Data. In 1997, Asian Americans made up nearly 6 percent of all students enrolled in higher education but only about 4 percent of the U.S. population. By education level, they accounted for 6 percent of all undergraduates, nearly 5 percent of graduate enrollment, and 22 percent of professional school enrollment. In contrast, the comparative percentages for other groups were as follows: whites, 70.5, 72.0, and 74.0 percent; African Americans, 11.0, 7.5, and 7.0 percent; Hispanics, 9.0, 4.5, and 5.0 percent; and American Indians, 1.5, 0.5, and less than 1 percent (Wilds, 2000).

Women in general are attending college in record numbers. Asian American women have made great strides over the past decade but lag behind women of other racial and ethnic groups. Women made up 51 percent of all Asian American students in 1997, somewhat less than for all students (56 percent) and for whites (56 percent) (Wilds, 2000).

In 1997, some 60.4 percent of Asian American undergraduates attended four-year institutions, with the remainder at two-year institutions, a consistent trend over the past decade. This is similar to all undergraduates (61 percent) and to whites (63 percent). Like other minority groups, the vast majority (79.2 percent) of Asian Americans are enrolled in public institutions (Wilds, 2000).

Degrees Earned. In 1997, Asian Americans earned 4.4 percent of all associate degrees, 5.8 percent of all bachelor's degrees, 4.5 percent of all master's degrees, and 9 percent of all first professional degrees (Wilds, 2000).

U.S. institutions educate foreign or international students, especially at the post-baccalaureate level, as well as U.S. citizens and residents. Foreign students earned 35 percent of all doctorates awarded in the United States in 1997. To more accurately measure the representation and progress (or lack of it) of Asian American students in the academic pipeline, institutions need to treat international students from Asia, the majority of whom return to their homelands, and Asian Americans, who are members of a U.S. racial minority group, as two distinct populations. For example, in 1997, Asian foreign students received 7,688 doctorates, or about 18 percent of all doctorates awarded in the United States. In contrast, Asian Americans earned 1,329 doctorates that year, or 3 percent of all doctoral degrees overall and 4.8 percent of all doctorates earned by U.S. citizens (Wilds, 2000).

Women in all racial and ethnic groups now earn more associate, bachelor's, and master's degrees than their male counterparts. Of all Asian American degrees in 1997, women obtained 57 percent of associate degrees, 53 percent of bachelor's degrees, and 54 percent of master's degrees. Men generally continue to earn more first professional and doctoral degrees than women. In 1997, Asian American women earned 46 percent of all Asian American first professional degrees, an increase from 37 percent in 1987, and 43 percent of all Asian American doctorates, up from 32 percent in 1987 (Wilds, 2000).

Fields of Study. In 1997, business was the leading field of study for all bachelor's degree recipients and for Asian American baccalaureates. By gender, it was followed by engineering, the biological and life sciences, and social sciences for Asian American men and biological and life sciences, the social sciences, and health professions for Asian American women. Education was the first choice of all master's degree students, followed by business. In contrast, Asian Americans chose business first, followed by engineering for male students and education and the health professions for female students. Education, followed closely by the life sciences and social sciences, led in doctorates earned by U.S. citizens, while Asian American doctorates chose the life sciences as their leading major, followed by engineering and the physical sciences (Wilds, 2000).

In summary, the Asian American population that has emerged through past and present immigration is fluid, complex, and heterogeneous. As the population increases largely through new immigration, the number of Asian American college students also grows. Their educational pipeline is not free-flowing, however. There are constrictions, especially by gender and at the doctoral level. Disparities also exist within the population by ethnic group. The interests and career goals of Asian American college students are complex and diverse as well. In many aspects, they resemble all students in the United States. In other areas, their educational status reflects family class background and level of acculturation, as well as racial and gender barriers in higher education (Hune, 1998; Hune and Chan, 1997).

Asian American educational data also have limitations. Data derived from the U.S. census are deceptive in conflating the human capital of Asian immigrants educated abroad with those schooled in the United States. Nonetheless, census data do disaggregate by Asian and Pacific Islander ethnic group and reveal significant differences within the API population. As other available data on Asian American students, notably institutional data, are generally aggregated, great care must be taken in interpreting them. Such data homogenize them and conceal individual and group distinctions that require attention.

Implications for Policies, Programs, and Services

The use of *Asian American* as an umbrella category in public policy is helpful, but it can obscure demographic differences that need to be addressed to benefit specific Asian and Pacific groups and individuals. Aggregated data suggest that Asian Americans are members of a "success story," while disaggregated U.S. census data challenge this notion by uncovering differences in ethnicity, income, education, family size, language proficiency, and other aspects. An understanding of Asian American college students as a diverse population with ethnic-specific and need-specific concerns can help higher education professionals serve them better.

National educational statistics are limited and may not reflect individual campus demographics. To develop appropriate policies, programs, and services for Asian American students, institutions need to collect both aggregate and ethnic-specific data on their Asian American campus population. Considering Asian foreign students and Asian Americans, a racial minority group, as two distinct populations with their own needs and concerns also can enhance services to both communities.

Statistics are only part of the story. In numerous qualitative studies, including campus diversity reports, Asian American students, faculty, and staff have documented their issues and voiced their neglect by professionals in higher education (Hune and Chan, 1997). Acknowledging the presence of Asian American students is not the same as recognizing their educational needs and concerns. Asian American students identify access and equity in academic and student services as issues along with a chilly classroom climate; racial and ethnic stereotyping by faculty, staff, and other students; and the lack of advisement and support for their integration into campus life (Osajima, 1995; Woo, 1997). Ethnic-specific and need-specific policies and programs may be required to enhance the academic progress of groups at risk, especially Southeast Asian and Pacific Islander groups. First-generation Asian American college students and those from low-income households are less familiar with U.S. institutions, values, and culture and seek support to negotiate college, where they feel like "outsiders." Students who have limited English or speak with an accent report language bias and discrimination and find they can be penalized academically. Female students, in particular, find barriers in the classroom and advisement and can experience sexual harassment. And racial incidents and hate crimes against Asian American students need to be taken seriously by higher education professionals (Hune, 1998).

Asian Americans are heterogeneous, and so are their educational needs. Their issues also change, reflecting the population's dynamics. Knowledge of Asian American demographics, diversity, and concerns can do much toward developing relevant higher education policies, programs, and services for Asian American students. Most important, student affairs professionals have a critical role to play in addressing and making visible the needs and concerns of Asian American college students.

References

Chan, S. *Asian Americans: An Interpretive History.* Boston: Twayne, 1991.

Espiritu, Y. L. *Asian American Panethnicity: Bridging Institutions and Identities.* Philadelphia: Temple University Press, 1992.

Espiritu, Y. L., and Omi, M. "'Who Are You Calling Asian?': Shifting Identity Claims, Racial Classifications, and the Census." In P. M. Ong (ed.), *Transforming Race Relations.* Los Angeles: LEAP Asian Pacific American Public Policy Institute and UCLA Asian American Studies Center, 2000.

Hune, S. *Asian Pacific American Women in Higher Education: Claiming Visibility and Voice.* Washington, D.C.: Association of American Colleges and Universities, 1998.

Hune, S., and Chan, K. S. "Special Focus: Asian Pacific American Demographic and Educational Trends." In D. J. Carter and R. Wilson (eds.), *Fifteenth Annual Status Report on Minorities in Higher Education, 1996–1997.* Washington, D.C.: American Council on Education, 1997.

Okihiro, G. Y. *Margins and Mainstreams.* Seattle: University of Washington Press, 1994.

Osajima, K. "Racial Politics and the Invisibility of Asian Americans in Higher Education." *Educational Foundations,* 1995, 9(1), 35–53.

Umemoto, K. "From Vincent Chin to Joseph Ileto: Asian Pacific Americans and Hate Crime Policy." In P. M. Ong (ed.), *Transforming Race Relations.* Los Angeles: LEAP Asian Pacific American Public Policy Institute and UCLA Asian American Studies Center, 2000.

U.S. Census Bureau. *1990 Census of Population, Social, and Economic Characteristics.* Washington, D.C.: U.S. Government Printing Office, 1993a.

U.S. Census Bureau. *We the American Asians, and We the American Pacific Islanders.* Washington, D.C.: U.S. Government Printing Office, 1993b.

U.S. Census Bureau. *Money Income in the United States, 1998.* Washington, D.C.: U.S. Government Printing Office, 1999.

U.S. Census Bureau. *Resident Population Estimates of the United States by Sex, Race, and Hispanic Origin.* Washington, D.C.: U.S. Government Printing Office, 2000.

Wei, W. *The Asian American Movement.* Philadelphia: Temple University Press, 1993.

Wilds, D. J. *Seventeenth Annual Status Report on Minorities in Higher Education, 1999–2000.* Washington, D.C.: American Council on Education, 2000.

Woo, D. *The Glass Ceiling and Asian Americans.* Washington, D.C.: U.S. Department of Labor, Glass Ceiling Commission, 1994.

Woo, D. "Asian Americans in Higher Education: Issues of Diversity and Engagement." *Race, Gender and Class,* 1997, 4(3), 122–143.

SHIRLEY HUNE *is professor of urban planning and associate dean for graduate programs in the Graduate Division, University of California, Los Angeles.*

3

The model minority stereotype of Asian Americans is retrospectively analyzed twenty-five years after the author's original study of the issue. The continuing effects of this stereotype in higher education are examined.

Revisiting the Model Minority Stereotype: Implications for Student Affairs Practice and Higher Education

Bob H. Suzuki

About twenty-five years ago, I published an article titled "Education and the Socialization of Asian Americans: A Revisionist Analysis of the 'Model Minority' Thesis" (Suzuki, 1977). The article debunked an increasingly pervasive stereotype emerging at the time of Asian Americans as a phenomenally successful, "problem-free" minority group that was, as one correspondent put it, "outwhiting whites" ("Success Story," 1971). In this chapter, I revisit my earlier analysis of the model minority stereotype through the perspective of the past twenty-five years, discussing what its impact has been and continues to be in higher education.

Negative Consequences of the Model Minority Stereotype

I was motivated to write my original article for two reasons. First, I was skeptical of the motives behind the sterling image of Asian Americans suddenly being projected by the media in the mid-1960s (Peterson, 1966; "Success Story," 1966). During the late 1800s and well into the 1940s, Asian Americans were generally portrayed as an invading "yellow peril," a horde of depraved, uncivilized heathens who threatened to undermine the American way of life (Miller, 1969; Ogawa, 1971). Even as recently as the early 1960s, Asian Americans were still portrayed quite negatively, either as obsequious, slavish, and subservient or as treacherous, deceitful, and untrustworthy. Even though by then many Asian Americans were third- or fourth-generation Americans, they still were viewed, more often than not, as foreigners, not as full-fledged Americans.

I was therefore quite suspicious of the sudden change in the image of Asian Americans and did not find it fortuitous that this change was occurring at a time when the country was facing a major crisis in race relations. Indeed, I agreed with the many Asian American social activists who charged that Asian Americans were being promoted as the model minority to discredit the protests and demands for social justice of other minority groups (Uyematsu, 1971; Wake, 1970).

My second reason for challenging the model minority stereotype was my growing concern with the negative consequences of this ostensibly positive image. Although Asian Americans were still facing many discriminatory barriers, especially in the area of employment, complaints about such discrimination were often not taken seriously and dismissed by employers as baseless. In fact, Asian Americans were initially not included as a protected minority group under federal affirmative action regulations. Moreover, government agencies and nonprofit organizations were not inclined to fund programs for Asian Americans in need of assistance because of the perception that the Asian communities had few, if any, problems, were self-sufficient, and "took care of their own."

Challenging the Model Minority Stereotype

For all these reasons, I decided to carry out some preliminary research that would challenge the model minority stereotype and lead to a very different interpretation of the available socioeconomic data on Asian Americans. By aggregating data on all of the Asian subgroups, earlier researchers had shown that Asian Americans as a single group appeared to be doing relatively well in comparison with other groups (Peterson, 1971; Urban Associates, 1974). For example, their analyses showed that Asian American families had a higher median annual income than U.S. families in general and that the median years of schooling completed by Asian Americans was higher than for the U.S. population as a whole. Such global and rather simplistic analyses were the basis for the model minority concept promoted by the media.

My initial analysis and subsequent studies by other researchers showed that when the socioeconomic data on Asian Americans were disaggregated and more sophisticated analyses conducted, a very different picture emerged. Such analyses showed that the median family income of Asian Americans was higher than that of white families because Asian American families had more earners contributing to family income and were concentrated in high-cost-of-living and high-income areas. When adjustments were made for these factors, the median family income of Asian Americans actually fell below that of white families. The analyses also showed that the annual per capita income of Asian Americans was considerably less than their white counterparts who had the same level of education, and the disparity was even greater when level of education and geographical area of residence was kept constant. And finally, they showed that the proportion of Asian Americans living below the poverty line was considerably higher than that of the white population (Cabezas, 1977; Chun, 1980; Suzuki, 1977). These findings clearly showed that Asian Americans still were struggling to achieve parity with their white counterparts.

Revisiting the Model Minority Stereotype

Have there been changes in the model minority stereotype of Asian Americans since these earlier findings twenty-five years ago? Certainly one change has been that in recent years, non–Asian American social scientists have been more hesitant about invoking the model minority stereotype in studies on Asian Americans, and the media have been less prone to promoting the stereotype. I believe this is due in part to the steady stream of publications by Asian American social scientists whose research has strongly validated the earlier findings that challenged the model minority myth (Jiobu, 1988; Nee and Sanders, 1985; Suzuki, 1989; Wong, 1982).

However, despite these findings, the perception is still widespread that Asian Americans have overcome all barriers of racial discrimination and are more successful even than whites. I believe this perception is due to several factors. First, a large proportion of Asian Americans graduate from college; in fact, the 1990 census showed that 38 percent of Asian Americans were college graduates, compared to 20 percent of the U.S. population as a whole (U.S. Census Bureau, 1993b). Moreover, the socioeconomic status of Asian Americans has also continued to rise since the 1970s. The 1990 census showed that the median family income of Asian Americans was higher than that of white families (U.S. Census Bureau, 1993b). In addition, the phenomenal rise of Japan and other Asian countries as major economic powers in the 1980s and the immigration of many wealthy Asians to the United States from these countries may contribute to the perception that Asian Americans are better off economically than whites (Stokes, 1987; Wallace, 1982). Even though such a relationship between the Asian countries and Asian Americans is tenuous at best, the public at large may find such a connection credible because of the tendency to view Asian Americans as foreigners and not as Americans (Tuan, 1998).

However, again, more in-depth analyses of the data tell a very different story. Since the late 1980s, several researchers have conducted detailed studies into the socioeconomic status of Asian Americans (Cabezas and Kawaguchi, 1988; Federal Glass Ceiling Commission, 1995; Hune and Chan, 1997; Jiobu, 1988; Wong and Nagasawa, 1991; Woo, 2000). Among many other findings, these studies showed that whites consistently gain a substantially higher return on education than any of the Asian American groups; that is, for the same level of education, whites are more likely to earn more, on the average, than Asian Americans. In addition, the poverty rate for Asian Americans still is considerably higher than that for whites. And finally, native-born Asian American men are less likely to be in management positions than their white counterparts, and highly educated native-born Asian American men are earning less—in most cases, considerably less—than similarly qualified white men. One study suggested that although their relatively high levels of education enabled Asian American men to enter high-paying occupations and industries, they encounter a racial barrier, the so-called glass ceiling, as they try to move upward (Woo, 2000).

Despite some disparities in the findings of these researchers, they have all concluded that as a group, Asian Americans have not yet achieved full equality and participation in American society. Although they are well educated and gain relatively easy access to entry-level jobs, they continue to face inequities in income and upward job mobility. However, the model minority stereotype has had the effect of glossing over these problems, making them easy to ignore or neglect.

Reemergence of the Perfidious Foreigner Stereotype

Paradoxically, even as the model minority stereotype continues to be perpetuated, the older stereotype of Asian Americans as the "perfidious foreigner" seems to be reemerging. This stereotype was reinforced strongly by U.S. propaganda during the Vietnam War. It was further reinforced in the 1980s when Japan and other Asian countries emerged as major economic powers and were viewed as a threat to U.S. dominance in the global economy. And during the past decade or so, with the end of the Cold War, China has replaced the Soviet Union as a major threat to the American way of life.

These developments may have set the stage for the most recent outbreak of xenophobia against Asian Americans. For example, in the mid-1990s, a scandal erupted over the donations made to the Clinton-Gore campaign by Asian Americans who, according to reports in the media, had close ties to various Asian countries, including Indonesia, Taiwan, and South Korea. Although such ties were never proved to exist, the matter became a major scandal, far out of proportion to the charges, and had the effect of raising suspicions about the loyalty of all Asian Americans (Lacey, 1997; Wu, 1996). Once again, Asian Americans were viewed as foreigners who could not be trusted because of their ethnic backgrounds and ties to Asian countries.

More recently, the specter of racial profiling of Asian Americans was raised by the arrest and imprisonment of Wen Ho Lee, a scientist at the Los Alamos National Laboratory, for allegedly stealing U.S. nuclear secrets and passing them on to an agent of China (Sheer, 2000). Asian American supporters of Lee, who rallied for his release, accused the government of targeting him because of his race and contended that he had been indicted and arrested on the flimsiest of evidence (Wise, 2000; Yin, 2000). Because of Lee's treatment and the increased security measures taken at Los Alamos,

Asian American scientists and engineers there were reportedly seeking jobs elsewhere, and job applications at the laboratory from Asian American scientists and engineers all but dried up (Glanz, 2000; McFarling, 2000).

Thus in retrospect, as we begin the twenty-first century, I believe the model minority stereotype is still alive and well. Although it is less flaunted by the media, its effects may be more insidious because it has become an almost unconscious image embedded in the minds of the public, subliminally influencing their perceptions. Worse yet, the perfidious foreigner stereotype has reared its ugly head again and, paradoxically, is working in tandem with the model minority stereotype to influence the public's perception of Asian Americans. Together, these stereotypes are pernicious in their impact on Asian Americans and, as I will discuss, are also influencing attitudes toward Asian Americans in our institutions of higher education.

Asian Americans in Higher Education

As the data presented in Chapter Two show, Asian Americans are well represented among students and faculty in higher education. In fact, in the fall of 1997, full-time Asian American faculty totaled 31,259, or 5 percent of all full-time faculty, outnumbering both African American and Hispanic full-time faculty ("Number of Full-Time Faculty Members," 2000). However, they are underrepresented severely in administrative positions and even fall far below the numbers of black and Hispanic administrators. In the fall of 1997, there were 2,736 Asian Americans in executive, administrative, or managerial positions, or about 2 percent of the total number ("Employees in Colleges and Universities," 2000). They were even more severely underrepresented among the chief executive officers of the over three thousand institutions of higher education in the United States, numbering around twenty-four, or only 0.8 percent of the total number ("Characteristics of College Presidents," 2000).

It should be noted that the aggregated data just presented conceal the tremendous diversity of the Asian American population in the United States. This population consists of at least thirty ethnic subgroups that differ enormously in cultural background, historical experience, and socioeconomic circumstances. For example, certain Southeast Asian subgroups, such as the Hmong and Cambodians, are still severely underrepresented in the student population and among the faculty of institutions of higher education and have much lower incomes and suffer much higher rates of poverty than other Asian American subgroups.

The Impact of Stereotyping on Asian Americans in Higher Education

The stereotyping of Asian Americans both as the model minority and as the perfidious foreigner has had invidious consequences for them in higher education. My discussion of these consequences will be based on three sources of information: (1) my many years of experience as a faculty member and administrator in several institutions of higher education, (2) two reports issued by the Asian Pacific American Education Advisory Committee in the California State University system in 1990 and 1994, and (3) other reports and studies on Asian Americans in higher education.

Let me begin with a personal anecdote. In the 1980s, when I was an administrator at another institution, I learned firsthand how damaging the model minority stereotype could be for Asian American students. This institution had an unusually large counseling center with around thirty professional counselors on its staff. However, not one of these counselors was Asian American, despite the fact that more than 15 percent of the student body was comprised of Asian Americans.

When I inquired into the situation, I was told that very few Asian American students used the services of the center, and the staff apparently concluded that Asian American students were so well adjusted and had so few personal problems that they had no need for psychological counseling. I questioned the validity of this conclusion and insisted that the center make greater efforts to hire an Asian American counselor.

My persistence on this matter over a two-year period finally resulted in the hiring of the first Asian American counselor by the center. In a matter of months, the new counselor was inundated with Asian American students seeking her advice on a wide range of psychological problems. By the end of the academic year, the backlog of students wishing to see her became so large that she was staying well into the evening hours to keep up with her workload. Finally, she told the center director that she was reaching a breaking point and appealed to him to either hire another Asian American counselor or allow her to cross-train a number of the other counselors.

They decided on the latter course of action, and subsequently, the Asian American counselor worked with several of the other counselors, familiarizing them with the typical problems faced by Asian American students and briefing them on how she advised these students. She then distributed her backlog to these other counselors, and much to their surprise, they discovered that they could be almost as effective in advising these students as the Asian American counselor. Although increasing the diversity of the counseling staff by only one person of Asian American background was by no means sufficient, the center was still able to improve the staff's capability, broaden the range of students they could serve, and thereby provide higher-quality service to students.

I believe that the counseling center was influenced strongly by the model minority stereotype. Asian American students have generally been stereotyped as superbright, highly motivated overachievers who come from well-to-do families. It may have been inconceivable to many of the center's staff that such students were encountering any serious psychological problems. Furthermore, the experience I have recounted is far from an isolated case. Several other Asian American counselors with whom I have talked have described similar experiences on their campuses.

These counselors, as well as Asian American psychologists who have conducted research in this area (Sue and Morishima, 1982; Sue and Zane, 1985), have reported that many Asian American students are experiencing extreme psychological stress and alienation. Because of the model minority stereotype, they are often subjected to unrealistically high expectations by their parents, their instructors, and even their peers. For a number of students, the pressures become so great that their academic performance suffers, forcing some of them to drop out of school. These psychological problems have been exacerbated by incidences of racial harassment and even violence against Asian American students on several campuses across the country (Asian-Pacific Advisory Committee, 1988; Clemetson, 2000). Unfortunately, because these problems go largely unrecognized by institutions of higher education, most Asian American students receive little, if any, help in coping with them.

The model minority stereotype also has other detrimental consequences for Asian Americans in higher education. A number of such consequences came to light through the work of the Asian Pacific American Education Advisory (APAEA) Committee of the California State University (CSU) system. This committee was established by the chancellor of the CSU system in 1989 to study the problems and needs of Asian Pacific Americans (APAs) on the CSU campuses. Because of the massive size of the CSU system and the fact that its APA enrollment in 1989 was about 11 percent of the total nationwide enrollment of APAs in higher education, I believe that many of the committee's findings and recommendations should have applicability beyond the CSU system.

A major unexpected finding of the committee was the dire need to provide assistance to Asian American students who did not speak English as their first language in developing their English communication skills. The CSU requires all students to pass a writing test as a requirement for graduation. During its public hearings, the committee heard from a number of Asian American English-as-a-second-language (ESL) students who recounted, some tearfully, their many attempts to pass this test, often delaying their graduation by one or two years. The committee also learned that only one or two CSU campuses provided these students with any assistance in this area. Other researchers have reported similar findings for Asian American ESL students in other parts of the country (Hsia, 1988; Tsuchida, 1982).

Asian American students and staff who appeared before the committee testified that the climate on the CSU campuses was not comfortable or inviting and that student service programs tended to exclude Asian American students and were indifferent to their problems and needs. Thus the committee found that "APA students, particularly those from underrepresented groups, are underserved by these programs and are often in dire need of assistance" (APAEA Committee, 1990, p. ix). Again, this problem is not unique to the CSU campuses but is reported on other campuses around the country as well (Greene, 1987).

Concern is also growing among Asian American students about subtle incidents of discrimination, such as derogatory remarks by instructors about the limited English proficiency of Asian American ESL students, covertly racist statements about Asian Americans by both instructors and students, and expressions of resentment by other students toward the achievement orientation of Asian American students (Loo and Rolison, 1986; APAEA Committee, 1990). Asian American students have also complained that many instructors do not trust them and unfairly accuse them of cheating on exams (APAEA Committee, 1990). What may be at work in these situations is not the model minority stereotype but the perfidious foreigner stereotype.

The committee's research showed that "although about 8 percent of the faculty and staff in the CSU were Asians, they tend to be concentrated in certain areas and are sparsely represented in other areas. APAs are especially underrepresented among . . . administrative/management employees, constituting less than 5 percent of such employees, and are practically nonexistent in higher level executive positions" (APAEA Committee, 1990, p. ix). Other studies have shown that Asian American students tend to major in science- and math-based fields and are less attracted to fields that require well-developed verbal or linguistic skills, such as education and the humanities (Hsia, 1988; Hune and Chan, 1997). Similar patterns exist among Asian American faculty (Vetter and Babco, 1987).

It is clear that Asian Americans are severely underrepresented in higher-level administrative positions in higher education. A number of studies have shown that Asian Americans are also underrepresented in management and leadership positions in all other sectors of our society (Jiobu, 1988; Kawaguchi and Cabezas, 1989; Woo, 2000). This "glass ceiling" barrier for Asian Americans is attributed primarily to racial discrimination. However, I believe that for Asian Americans, racial discrimination takes particularly subtle forms and is due to the stereotyping of them both as the model minority and as the perfidious foreigner. Because Asian American students are viewed as "problem-free" high achievers, they have not been encouraged or assisted in developing their verbal and linguistic skills. Moreover, the underdevelopment of these skills also hinders their ability to assume leadership roles in student organizations, affecting them later as they pursue professional careers. And as Asian Americans strive for upward mobility in their careers, they are viewed as lacking the requisite skills to be effective leaders and are therefore often passed up for management positions. The few who achieve management and other leadership roles are often viewed suspiciously as untrustworthy because of the stereotypical image of them as the perfidious foreigner. These stereotypes working in tandem make it doubly difficult for Asian Americans to be selected for these roles and, when selected, to succeed in these roles.

The APAEA Committee (1990) made special note in its report of the fact that "although APA students as a group appear to be well represented on all CSU campuses, particular subpopulations of APAs, such as Southeast

Asians and Pacific Islanders, are still underrepresented. These students are underserved by campus outreach and admissions programs and are generally not included as a targeted group by these programs" (p. ix). Moreover, these groups are even more severely underrepresented among the faculty and staff.

The committee's most general overall finding was that the CSU campuses had "largely overlooked the problems and needs of APA students due in part to the widespread acceptance of the model minority stereotype" and had not "adequately responded to their growing presence and diversity" (p. ix). If this situation exists in the state with the largest APA population, it can likely be generalized to other institutions throughout the country.

Summary and Recommendations

The model minority and perfidious foreigner stereotypes have had detrimental consequences for Asian Americans in higher education. On the one hand, because Asian American students are stereotyped as "problem-free" high achievers, institutions of higher education have tended to neglect and ignore the many serious problems and needs they have. On the other hand, because Asian Americans also are stereotyped as untrustworthy "foreigners," Asian American students often encounter racial harassment or are suspected of cheating. Through similar stereotyping, Asian American faculty and administrators are viewed as unsuited for higher-level leadership roles. In the face of such stereotyping, what can student affairs practitioners do to help address the problems and needs of Asian Americans in higher education? I suggest the following concrete steps.

- Conduct workshops, retreats, and other activities for students, faculty, administrators, and staff on diversity and multiculturalism, including segments on the stereotyping of Asian Americans and its damaging effects. Because attitudes and behaviors change very slowly, these activities should not be one-shot efforts but should be conducted on an ongoing basis.
- Establish a campuswide committee to monitor incidents of racial harassment, with particular attention given to Asian American students, who are often not perceived as victims of such harassment and may not speak out about it. This committee should also work with institutional leaders to develop and implement strategies for improving the campus climate.
- Support efforts to diversify the staffs of student affairs units, including efforts to recruit Asian Americans for such positions, especially on campuses with significant numbers of Asian American students, and provide training to student affairs practitioners on effective approaches to working with Asian American students.
- Provide assistance to Asian American and other ESL students to enable them to develop their English communication skills to a level necessary for college work.

- Offer workshops, conferences, and other activities to develop the leadership skills of Asian American and other minority students who tend not to be involved in mainstream student organizations and to increase their involvement in these organizations.
- Provide opportunities for Asian American student affairs staff to develop their leadership skills by assigning them leadership roles, supporting their attendance at seminars and conferences,[1] and offering other professional development activities. Because they perceive that a glass ceiling blocks their advancement, these Asian American staff members are often reluctant to apply for higher-level administrative positions but should be encouraged to do so.
- Include certain Asian American subpopulations, such as the various Southeast Asian groups who are still underrepresented in higher education, in outreach and admissions efforts to recruit a more diverse student body and in educational equity programs to provide them with financial aid and other supportive services to help them succeed academically.

Conclusion

Due to limitations of space, this retrospective review of the model minority stereotype and the issues facing Asian Americans in higher education was not meant to be exhaustive. I have tried to cover only the issues that I thought would be of greatest interest to student affairs practitioners and have not included others, such as those related to curriculum and instruction, which are not in the direct purview of student affairs. Nevertheless, I hope that a sufficiently comprehensive overview was provided to stimulate the further thought and discussion needed to develop and implement student affairs programs that address the problems and needs of Asian Americans and other minorities in higher education.

Note

1. A seminar on leadership development for Asian American faculty and administrators, many of them in the area of student affairs, has been offered at California State Polytechnic University, Pomona, for about four years. This seminar has been conducted by an organization called Leadership Education for Asian Pacifics (LEAP), headquartered in Los Angeles.

References

Asian-Pacific Advisory Committee. *Final Report.* Sacramento, Calif.: Office of the Attorney General, 1988.
Asian Pacific American Education Advisory Committee. *Enriching California's Future: Asian Pacific Americans in the CSU.* Long Beach: California State University, 1990.
Asian Pacific American Education Advisory Committee. *Asian Pacific Americans in the CSU: A Follow-Up Report.* Long Beach: California State University, 1994.
Cabezas, A. Y. "A View of Poor Linkages Between Education, Occupation, and Earnings

for Asian Americans." Paper presented at the Third National Forum on Education and Work, San Francisco, 1977.

Cabezas, A. Y., and Kawaguchi, G. "Empirical Evidence for Continuing Asian American Income Inequality: The Human Capital Model and Labor Market Segmentation." In G. Y. Okihiro, S. Hune, A. A. Hansen, and J. M. Liu (eds.), *Reflections on Shattered Windows: Promises and Prospects for Asian American Studies.* Pullman: Washington State University Press, 1988.

"Characteristics of College Presidents, 1995." *Chronicle of Higher Education,* Sept. 1, 2000, p. 38.

Chun, K. T. "The Myth of Asian American Success and Its Educational Ramifications." *IRCD Bulletin,* 1980, *1 and 2,* 1–12. Reprinted in D. T. Nakanishi and T. Y. Nishida (eds.), *The Asian American Educational Experience: A Source Book for Teachers and Students.* New York: Routledge, 1995.

Clemetson, L. "The New Victims of Hate: Bias Crimes Hit America's Fastest-Growing Ethnic Group." *Newsweek,* Nov. 6, 2000, p. 61.

"Employees in Colleges and Universities by Racial and Ethnic Group, Fall 1997." *Chronicle of Higher Education,* Sept. 1, 2000, p. 38.

Federal Glass Ceiling Commission. *Good for Business: Making Full Use of the Nation's Human Capital.* Washington, D.C.: U.S. Government Printing Office, 1995.

Glanz, J. "Amid Race Profiling Claims, Asian-Americans Avoid Labs." *New York Times,* July 16, 2000, p.1.

Greene, E. "Asian-Americans Find U.S. Colleges Insensitive, Form Campus Organizations to Fight Bias." *Chronicle of Higher Education,* Nov. 18, 1987, pp. A1, A38–40.

Hsia, J. *Asian Americans in Higher Education and at Work.* Mahwah, N.J.: Erlbaum, 1988.

Hune, S., and Chan, K. S. "Special Focus: Asian Pacific American Demographic and Educational Trends." In D. J. Carter and R. Wilson (eds.), *Fifteenth Annual Status Report on Minorities in Higher Education, 1996–1997.* Washington, D.C.: American Council on Education, 1997.

Jiobu, R. M. *Ethnicity and Assimilation: Blacks, Chinese, Filipinos, Japanese, Koreans, Mexicans, Vietnamese, and White.* Albany: State University of New York Press, 1988.

Kawaguchi, G., and Cabezas, A. Y. "Errors of Commission: The U.S. Commission on Civil Rights Report on the Economic Status of Americans of Asian Descent." Paper presented at the Sixth National Conference of the Association of Asian American Studies, Hunter College, City University of New York, June 1989.

Lacey, M. "Parties Exchange Charges at Hearing on Anti-Asian Bias." *Los Angeles Times,* Dec. 6, 1997, p. 20.

Loo, C., and Rolison, G. "Alienation of Ethnic Minority Students at a Predominantly White University." *Journal of Higher Education,* 1986, *57,* 58–77.

McFarling, U. L. "Case's Legacy Is Distrust in Scientific Community." *Los Angeles Times,* Sept. 14, 2000, p. A16.

Miller, S. C. *The Unwelcome Immigrant: The American Image of the Chinese, 1785–1882.* Berkeley: University of California Press, 1969.

Nee, V., and Sanders, J. "The Road to Parity: Determinants of the Socioeconomic Achievement of Asian Americans." *Ethnic and Racial Studies,* 1985, *28,* 281–306.

"Number of Full-Time Faculty Members by Sex, Rank, and Racial and Ethnic Group." *Chronicle of Higher Education,* Sept. 1, 2000, p. 38.

Ogawa, D. *From Japs to Japanese: The Evolution of Japanese-American Stereotypes.* Berkeley, Calif.: McCutchan, 1971.

Peterson, W. "Success Story: Japanese-American Style." *New York Times Magazine,* Jan. 9, 1966, p. 21.

Peterson, W. *Japanese Americans: Oppression and Success.* New York: Random House, 1971.

Sheer, R. "Spy Case Is Evaporating, but Not the Bad Smell." *Los Angeles Times,* July 11, 2000, p. B9.

Stokes, B. "New Rivals in Asia." *National Journal,* May 9, 1987, p. 1116.

"Success Story of One Minority Group in the U.S." *U.S. News & World Report,* Dec. 26, 1966, pp. 73–76.

"Success Story: Outwhiting the Whites." *Newsweek,* June 21, 1971, pp. 24–25.

Sue, S., and Morishima, J. K. *The Mental Health of Asian Americans.* San Francisco: Jossey-Bass, 1982.

Sue, S., and Zane, N.W.S. "Academic Achievement and Socioemotional Adjustment Among Chinese University Students." *Journal of Counseling Psychology,* 1985, *32,* 570–579.

Suzuki, B. H. "Education and the Socialization of Asian Americans: A Revisionist Analysis of the 'Model Minority' Thesis." *Amerasia Journal,* 1977, *4*(2), 23–51. Reprinted in D. T. Nakanishi and T. Y. Nishida (eds.), *The Asian American Educational Experience: A Source Book for Teachers and Students.* New York: Routledge, 1995.

Suzuki, B. H. "Asian Americans as the 'Model Minority': Outdoing Whites? Or Media Hype?" *Change,* Nov.-Dec. 1989, pp. 13–19.

Tsuchida, N. "Support Services and Academic Retention Programs for Indochinese Students at the University of Minnesota." *Alternative Higher Education,* 1982, *6,* 160–171.

Tuan, M. *Forever Foreigners or Honorary Whites? The Asian Ethnic Experience Today.* New Brunswick, N.J.: Rutgers University Press, 1998.

Urban Associates, Inc. *A Study of Selected Socio-Economic Characteristics of Ethnic Minorities Based on the 1970 Census, II: Asian Americans.* Washington, D.C.: Office of Special Concerns, Department of Health, Education and Welfare, 1974.

Uyematsu, A. "The Emergence of Yellow Power in America." In A. Tachiki (ed.), *Roots: An Asian American Reader.* Los Angeles: UCLA Asian American Studies Center, 1971.

Vetter, B. M., and Babco, E. L. *Professional Women and Minorities: A Manpower Data Resource Service.* (7th ed.) Washington, D.C.: Scientific Manpower Commission, 1987.

Wake, L. "Shhh! An Asian American Is Speaking." *Hokubei Mainichi,* Feb. 1970.

Wallace, J. "The Festering Irritation with Japan." *U.S. News & World Report,* Aug. 23, 1982, p. 39.

Wise, D. "Lee's Free, but Mystery Remains." *Los Angeles Times,* Sept. 17, 2000, p. M1.

Wong, M. G. "The Cost of Being Chinese, Japanese, and Filipino in the United States, 1960, 1970, 1976." *Pacific Sociological Review,* 1982, *25,* 59–78.

Wong, P., and Nagasawa, R. "Asian American Scientists and Engineers: Is There a Glass Ceiling for Career Advancement?" *Chinese American Forum,* 1991, *6,* 307–338.

Woo, D. *Glass Ceilings and Asian Americans: The New Face of Workplace Barriers.* Walnut Creek, Calif.: Altamira Press, 2000.

Wu, F. H. "The John Huang Affair." *Asian Week,* Nov. 1–7, 1996, p. 11.

Yin, X. "The Lee Case Shakes Asian Americans' Faith in Justice System." *Los Angeles Times,* Sept. 24, 2000, p. M1.

BOB H. SUZUKI *is president of the California State Polytechnic University, Pomona.*

Racial identity is an important but often overlooked aspect of working with Asian American college students. An understanding of racial identity theory can provide useful insight into the ways students experience and deal with college experiences, peers, and their identity.

Racial Identity and Asian Americans: Supports and Challenges

Alvin N. Alvarez

From the Thai American student coordinating an Asian American heritage celebration to the Japanese American student who prefers to distance herself from Asian American student groups to the South Asian student grappling with a newfound awareness of racism in his Asian American history course, the varied faces of "Asian American racial identity" clearly challenge student affairs practitioners to recognize yet another level of heterogeneity in the Asian American student community. While various authors (Chun, 1980; Suzuki, 1977) have argued convincingly for recognition of the ethnic, generational, socioeconomic, and linguistic heterogeneity of the Asian American community, the concept of an Asian American racial identity has generally been treated as a homogenous construct, as though all Asian Americans identify psychologically with the Asian American community to the same degree. Even a cursory poll of Asian American students about Asian American racial identity will most likely yield a continuum of reactions, ranging from pride to confusion to outright rejection of such an identity. Consequently, a challenge for student affairs professionals in serving such a heterogeneous community is to address critical questions about the role of racial identity development for Asian American students—for instance: How is it that some students develop their racial and political consciousness whereas others do not? What facilitates this process of racial consciousness? And what role do student affairs professionals play in the development of an Asian American racial identity? The purpose of this chapter is to examine the relevance of race and racial identity for Asian Americans in college as well as their implications for student affairs professionals.

New Directions for Student Services, no. 97, Spring 2002 © Wiley Periodicals, Inc.

Obtaining an understanding of the role of race and racial identity in the lives of Asian American college students has been complicated by both conceptual imprecisions and empirical neglect. Kohatsu (1992) noted that in the case of Asian Americans, conceptual imprecisions have resulted in the treatment of racial identity, ethnic identity, and acculturation as interchangeable constructs. Hence, in line with the need for greater conceptual rigor, explicit definitions may be helpful in providing clarity for the reader. For the purposes of this chapter, *ethnicity* refers to Asian ethnic groups, such as Chinese, Pilipino, and Vietnamese (Ancheta, 1998), and by extension, *ethnic identity* refers to the quality of a person's identification with such groups. In contrast, *racial identity* refers to the quality of a person's identification with Asians and Asian Americans as a larger collective inclusive of the various ethnic groups (Ancheta, 1998; Espiritu, 1992). *Acculturation* refers to an identification with the norms, values, and beliefs of the dominant culture. Helms and Cook (1999) have suggested further that to the extent that a theory addresses individuals' intrapsychic and interpersonal reactions to racism, such a model might be better described as a *racial identity* theory; conversely, insofar as a theory focuses on the acquisition and retention of the values, beliefs, languages, and traditions of ethnic groups, such a model might be better described as a model of *ethnic identity*.

It is striking to note that researchers have generally neglected to examine the racial experiences of Asian Americans in college. With few exceptions (Alvarez and Yeh, 1999; Bagasao, 1989; Osajima, 1993), the psychological literature on Asian Americans has focused on issues such as adjustment patterns, underutilization of mental health services, and counselor preference (Uba, 1994). As Helms (2000) has noted, with regard to Asian Americans, researchers have typically focused on variables related to ethnicity and culture (for example, Sue, Mak, and Sue, 1998) and given relatively minimal attention to understanding how Asian Americans internalize and cope with race and racism.

Although the paucity of literature would seem to imply that racial issues are not salient to Asian Americans, Alvarez and Yeh (1999) observed that the activities of Asian American college students suggest that issues of race and racism may be prominent features in their lives. For instance, in the classroom, Asian American studies instructors have challenged students to examine the historical and sociopolitical contexts underlying the racial experiences of their communities. Outside the classroom, sociopolitical Asian American student coalitions have become visible catalysts in establishing Asian American programs (Monaghan, 1999) as well as advocating for the recruitment and retention of Asian American faculty, staff, and students and the expansion of services for Asian Americans.

Moving beyond the confines of individual institutions, regional Asian American student organizations and sizable student attendance at Asian American studies conferences have become common avenues for student empowerment and education. On a more somber note, highly publicized incidents of anti-Asian violence, harassment, and vandalism at various campuses (for example, University of California, Irvine; Stanford University; University of Connecticut; University of Illinois at Urbana-Champaign) (Alvarez and Yeh, 1999) have underscored the significance of race and racism for Asian American students.

However, issues of race and racism may not be equally salient for all segments of the Asian American student community (Alvarez and Yeh, 1999). While some Asian American students are passionate about taking pride in their racial identity, other students may regard such racial pride as a divisive and contentious political stance. For some Asian American students, issues of race and racism may be regarded as peripheral to both their daily lives and their identity. Yet in light of Alvarez and Yeh's contention that college can be a critical catalyst in challenging such color-blind racial views, student affairs practitioners may need to examine the developmental and psychological implications of race and racism (Young and Takeuchi, 1998) in order to understand the within-group differences in Asian American student communities.

A review of racial identity theory (Cross, 1971; Helms, 1995) as it relates to Asian American students may serve as a first step in addressing the implications of race and racism for student development. Racial identity theory explicitly addresses the manner in which individuals internalize and reexamine their experiences regarding race and racism. I have elected to review Helms's People of Color racial identity model (1995) as a conceptual framework for examining the racial identity development of Asian Americans in college.

Racial Identity Theory

According to Helms and Cook (1999), racial identity models describe interpersonal and intrapsychic reactions "for overcoming internalized racism and achieving a healthy socioracial self-conception under varying conditions of racial oppression" (p. 81). Theoretically, this developmental process involves progression through qualitatively distinct statuses of racial identity, each of which is characterized by unique cognitive, affective, and behavioral responses to race and race-related information. Recognizing the tendency of researchers and practitioners to categorize individuals into one status of identity, Helms (1995) has cautioned that such a practice may oversimplify the developmental process, since pure forms of each status are highly unlikely. Rather, she suggests that a racial identity profile consisting of multiple and interrelated racial identity statuses may be a more accurate description of an individual's racial identity development. Nevertheless, she does acknowledge that individuals may have a "dominant" status of racial identity for processing racial information.

A basic premise of racial identity theory is that psychological well-being is enhanced by a person's progression through increasingly mature statuses of racial identity (Cross, 1991; Helms, 1990). This developmental process involves maturation from the least sophisticated statuses of identity, characterized by racial naiveté and trivialization, to the more sophisticated statuses of identity, characterized by conscious racial self-affirmation. In her People of Color racial identity model, Helms (1995) outlined six statuses of racial identity development for African, Asian, Latino, and Native Americans in the United States: Conformity, Dissonance, Immersion, Emersion, Internalization, and Integrative Awareness. Although the specific histories of each socioracial group differ in content, Helms argued that the similarities in each community's experiences with racial oppression may result in similar processes of racial identity development (Helms and Cook, 1999). However, student affairs practitioners should also be mindful of how Asian cultural variables (for example, expression of emotion, shame, and self-disclosure) may influence the process of developing an Asian American racial identity (Alvarez and Kimura, 2001).

To facilitate the shift from theory to practice, Sanford's concept of "challenge and support" (1966) is helpful in exploring what constitutes developmentally appropriate challenges and supports for particular statuses of Asian American racial identity. Hence it is possible for practitioners to design programs, exercises, lectures, and activities that provide a developmentally appropriate degree of challenge and support for students, insofar as students operate from one or more identifiable statuses of identity. Although the intent of this chapter is not to provide a prescription for racial identity interventions, it is intended to encourage practitioners to begin considering the practical applications of racial identity theory.

Conformity. As the least sophisticated status of racial identity, Conformity is characterized by a trivialization or minimization of race and racial dynamics. With such a color-blind racial perspective, activities, discussions, and issues involving race may be anxiety-provoking for students operating from this worldview. Adopting a Conformity worldview also involves an Internalization of the values, norms, and beliefs of the dominant culture and a devaluation of Asian Americans and Asian culture, values, and norms. As a result, Asian American students with Conformity as their dominant identity status may idealize or attempt to assimilate into the white campus community while simultaneously rejecting any affiliation with other Asian or Asian American students and their organizations. Alvarez and Yeh (1999) observed that Conformity worldviews may be typical of Asian American students entering college, particularly students raised in environments with minimal contact or exposure to other Asian Americans.

A challenge for Asian American students who operate primarily from a Conformity worldview may occur as their color-blind perspective begins to conflict with college experiences that suggest that racial differences exist and that people may be treated differentially on the basis of race. In particular, events and activities that underscore "racial conflicts" (ethnoviolence and harassment) may be a direct challenge to a person's need to maintain a racial view of the world as harmonious and conflict-free (Alvarez and Kimura, 2001). Given that the Conformity status is characterized by an individual's assimilation of white cultural norms, students may also be challenged by experiences that suggest that whites still regard them as Asian Americans, despite their best efforts at assimilation. Conversely, association with other Asian Americans, particularly those who are vocal about issues of race and culture, may be uncomfortable. In effect, a primary challenge to a person's Conformity worldview may be the growing recognition that race, particularly one's own, is salient.

In contrast, support for a person operating from a Conformity worldview may be provided by validating a student's hope in a socially just world where race is not equated with differential treatment. For Asian American students who were raised in predominantly white neighborhoods, endorsement of a Conformity worldview may reflect both a means of survival and the absence of alternative worldviews. Recognizing Conformity as one form of adaptation to a dominant white culture, it may be important for practitioners to validate and empathize with students' desire to fit in with their environment as well as their lack of racial or cultural exposure. Consequently, exposure to the positive elements of Asian American communities, history, and culture may be a developmentally appropriate and nonthreatening method of introducing students to the significance of race and culture.

Dissonance. The development of the Dissonance status of racial identity begins to evolve as Asian American students continue to encounter experiences that suggest that race may be related to the differential treatment of both themselves and others. As their color-blind racial views are challenged, students may begin to question their idealization of white individuals and white culture as well as their denigration of Asian Americans and Asian culture. Hence it is not surprising that anxiety, confusion, and racial ambivalence are characteristics of the Dissonance status. For Asian American students who enter college operating primarily from a Conformity worldview, the full spectrum of Asian American student organizations, student protests, Asian American studies courses, and cultural celebrations may be catalysts for a reexamination of their color-blind views on race. Conversely, events that begin to challenge a student's idealization of white individuals and white culture—such as witnessing acts of overt white racism, being the object of racial stereotypes, and gaining an awareness of Eurocentrism—may be equally powerful catalysts (Alvarez and Kimura, 2001). In effect, college itself may be a Dissonance-inducing environment that underscores the salience of race and perhaps the value of identifying oneself in racial terms (Alvarez and Yeh, 1999).

The significant affective and cognitive challenges of Dissonance come as a result of racial experiences that disrupt a student's racial naiveté. In shifting away from a color-blind belief system, the scope of students' racial reevaluation may be both extensive and overwhelming as they begin to question race-related events and interactions. For instance, students may reassess relationships with their peers, family, and teachers, as well as the implicit and explicit racial messages conveyed by these individuals about the value (or lack thereof) of identifying oneself racially. Similarly, it may be psychologically painful for students to begin to recognize and acknowledge the previously denied racial significance of both past and current events—for example, verbal harassment, social exclusion, and being regarded as a foreigner.

In light of the ambivalence and confusion that characterizes this newly "awakened" racial consciousness, student affairs professionals may need to support Asian American students by validating their feelings of anxiety, confusion, and perhaps even a sense of disillusionment associated with the loss of their idealized view of the world. Students may also benefit from an environment that facilitates their newfound curiosity about issues and activities related to race and culture. Yet given the ambivalence and uncertainty that characterizes Dissonance, it is equally crucial that student affairs practitioners assist students in maintaining the fine balance between appropriate and overwhelming racial exposure. For instance, it may be more appropriate to involve students in an exercise that explores the positive influence of Asian culture on their family rather than an emotionally provocative exercise that explores their experiences with racism. Thus student affairs practitioners need to be mindful that the fragility of this developmental status can lead to racial identity regression or foreclosure as well as progression.

Immersion and Emersion. According to Helms (1995), the Immersion and Emersion statuses develop in response to the anxiety and confusion generated by the Dissonance status as well as a growing awareness of racial dynamics and hierarchies that relegate Asian Americans to positions of inferiority. As a result, the Immersion status is reflected in students' need to replace a white-imposed definition of themselves and their group with a positive, racially affirming self-definition coupled with an active exploration of Asian American history, culture, and values. Cognitively, the Immersion status is also characterized by a dualistic racial worldview based on an idealization of all aspects of Asian or Asian American culture and a denigration of all white individuals and white culture. The Emersion status is characterized by a sense of communality and solidarity with Asian Americans and support for Asian American–related issues. Hence enrollment in Asian American studies courses, protests in support of Asian American studies, involvement in the Asian community, and exclusive affiliation with Asian Americans and other people of color with similar political philosophies may all be characteristic of students as they reclaim and redefine their racial identity as Asian Americans. In light of such racial worldviews, the emotional intensity of the Immersion and Emersion statuses may range from euphoria and pride in Asian Americans to anger and hostility toward whites.

Questioning their idealization of Asian Americans and their reactionary denigration of white people as well as disrupting the cognitive rigidity associated with their polarized racial views may be particularly challenging for

Asian American students operating from the Immersion and Emersion statuses. Given the emotional charge that permeates the racial views of both statuses, students may find it challenging to begin to consider that all things Asian may not be good and that all things white may not be bad. For instance, students at this point in their development may find it difficult to accept white individuals who express support for the students' political beliefs and activities. Conversely, it may be equally challenging to a person's Immersion attitudes to empathize or express patience with peers, particularly if they are Asian American, who may not support Asian American–related issues. In light of their commitment to challenging the status quo, students may find it difficult to maintain their patience with a long-term process of change, particularly if it requires tolerating or working within the very institutions they are trying to reform, such as higher education.

Support for a student's Immersion and Emersion attitudes involves the recognition that with an awakening to sociopolitical oppression comes an intensity of emotions as well as a desire to challenge the perceived sources of oppression. As Asian American students explore and expand their knowledge of topics such as Asian American history, the dynamics of racism, and the disempowerment of people of color, student affairs professionals have the potential to normalize students' thirst for more exposure to such topics as well as the feelings of anger, resentment, and perhaps betrayal they may feel for having been "cheated" out of this information. Exposure to such information may be an impetus for Asian American students to change existing conditions (for example, curriculum, schools, neighborhoods) and to enlighten individuals who are perceived as being "unaware." While student affairs professionals can certainly provide validation for these goals, it is critical to assist students in expressing these goals in constructive rather than destructive ways. Hence practitioners may need to impart students with an understanding of the role of strategy in an activist agenda as well as recognition of the interpersonal, academic, and occupational consequences of their activism. For instance, Asian American students may need support in coping with the possibility of being isolated from and misunderstood by family, peers, teachers, and administrators who regard their passion for their community and their political views as overly hostile and radical.

Internalization. The Internalization status of racial identity evolves as individuals begin to reassess the affective intensity and dualistic racial views of the Immersion and Emersion statuses. In contrast to the cognitive rigidity of Immersion and Emersion, the Internalization status is defined by an individual's beginning attempt to develop a personally meaningful definition of an Asian American identity, rather than conforming to a group definition of what constitutes a "good" Asian American. In asserting this autonomy, individuals may struggle to maintain a healthy balance between personal and group definitions of one's identity as an Asian American. As a result, this status may be a reflective period in which Asian Americans begin to assess objectively both the strengths and the limitations of their own communities as well as those of the dominant racial group.

In developing a personally meaningful definition of their race, Asian American students may be challenged by attempts to objectively evaluate both Asian culture and the dominant white culture. This may involve a reevaluation of their idealized perceptions of Asian Americans as well as their generalizations about white people and white culture. As a result of this objectivity and reflection, a student's willingness to question and explore what it means to be an Asian American may be regarded as a deviation from or a betrayal of his or her former pro-Asian beliefs. Movement away from the intensity of the Immersion and Emersion statuses may be perceived by the individuals themselves and perhaps by other Asian Americans as a loss of their convictions. Subsequently, students may require the support of student affairs professionals in demonstrating their commitment to Asian American issues in a manner that is meaningful personally while resisting the pressure to conform to externally imposed definitions of what constitutes a "good Asian American student activist." Subsequently, practitioners can affirm the belief that differences in students' racial worldviews may exist without necessarily compromising their commitment to Asian Americans as a community.

Integrative Awareness. The most mature status of racial identity, the Integrative Awareness status is defined by a sense of racial self-esteem rooted in a self-affirming definition of oneself as an Asian American. Theoretically, individuals whose racial worldviews are characterized by the Integrative Awareness status have developed a definition of what it means to be an Asian American that integrates both personal and group definitions of that identity. Moreover, the Integrative Awareness status is also characterized by an integration of one's racial identity with other reference group identities—gender, sexual orientation, and socioeconomic status—into a holistic concept of self that is inclusive of the various facets of one's personhood.

Thus as students begin to operate from an Integrative Awareness perspective, an initial challenge may be to explore previously unexamined aspects of their identity (gender, sexual orientation, religion, physical abilities) while venturing away from the psychological familiarity and security of defining oneself in racial terms. Particularly in a society that prefers to categorize individuals unidimensionally, maintaining and affirming a multidimensional identity may be an ongoing challenge. Insofar as this exploration may lead to an awareness of areas of privilege in other domains of one's identity, the exploration may be particularly challenging. For instance, an Asian American man whose racial self-concept is rooted in the belief that he is oppressed racially may find it challenging to integrate his racial identity with his gender identity, insofar as gender identity development requires an awareness of his privileged position as a man. To aid in this process, student affairs professionals may facilitate students' self-exploration by challenging students to recognize the value of other aspects of their identity beyond race. Introducing students, either personally or through books or film, to Asian Americans who are able to integrate their racial identities with their gender, sexual orientation, and social class identities may be facilitative.

Implications for Student Affairs

While racial identity theory provides practitioners with a much needed framework for conceptualizing how Asian Americans attend to and cope with racial issues, the value of such a theory can also be measured by its utility to both student affairs professionals and students. As Evans, Forney, and Guido-DiBrito (1998) observed, "To be of any utility, theory must be related to practical situations found in real-life settings" (p. 19).

As a developmental model, the concepts of change and growth lie at the heart of racial identity theory. That is, there is an assumption that change, from racial naiveté to racial awareness, is not only desirable but also possible. In grappling with an issue as potentially contentious and divisive as race, an understanding that such change is possible may be instrumental in helping students cope with the frustration associated with a seemingly intractable issue. For instance, Asian American student leaders may express a sense of resentment regarding the perceived political apathy of their Asian American peers. Yet upon closer examination, this sense of resentment often reflects both a resigned assumption that such "apathy" is fixed combined with an uncertainty about how to effect change in their peers' racial views. Perhaps with a better understanding of racial identity theory and its developmental assumptions, student affairs practitioners can assist Asian American students in recognizing that change is possible, albeit gradual, even around an issue as complicated as race.

Racial identity theory also provides both students and practitioners with a framework for understanding how such changes might occur. For Asian American students, the goal of developing one's racial identity can be an ambiguous and emotionally evocative process. Students may grapple with both their own questions and the questions and concerns of their family and peers about what constitutes normality and health as they challenge and reexamine their views on race, racial issues, and their perceptions of self and others. For instance, one Chinese American student, frustrated by his roommate's strident political activism, challenged him by asking, "How come you've got to be angry all the time about this stuff?" It stands to reason that without a framework and language to describe this developmental process, such questions, from oneself and others, may exacerbate an already confusing period of transition. Racial identity theory, however, can provide students with both validation and clarity about the process of developing an Asian American racial identity and the range of cognitive, affective, and behavioral reactions associated with this process.

Given the interpersonal tension that may be associated with discussions on race, Helms (1990) has suggested in her interaction model that interpersonal dynamics in discussions and interactions around issues of race may be reflective of differences in the racial identity statuses of the individuals. For example, tension and conflict may result from an interaction between an individual whose racial views are based on the racial assertiveness of the

Immersion status and an individual who operates primarily from the color-blind views of the Conformity status. In contrast, two Asian American students operating from similar racial identity statuses will be more likely to express support for each other while experiencing minimal conflict in discussions around race and racial issues. Hence racial identity theory may provide both students and student affairs practitioners with a framework for understanding the interpersonal dynamics elicited by racial issues and how their own views on race and racism may contribute to such dynamics. Moreover, insofar as effective program planning, curriculum design, and group processing rely on the ability to anticipate the reactions of groups and individuals, racial identity theory may enable practitioners to prepare for, rather than be surprised by, the interpersonal dynamics elicited by race and race-related issues.

The developmental emphasis of racial identity theory may be useful in recognizing that process can be as central to an Asian American activist agenda as task. All too often, both student affairs practitioners and Asian American student leaders focus their time and energy on achieving particular tasks (for example, establishing an Asian American studies program; building a resource center; hiring an Asian American dean, psychologist, or instructor) while neglecting the developmental needs of a larger Asian American student community that remains unconvinced, if not unsupportive, of the significance of such goals. While institutional and structural reforms around curriculum, personnel recruitment, and student services are clearly valuable goals of student activism, facilitating the developmental growth of a community may be an equally valuable yet often overlooked goal. If Asian American student leaders and student affairs professionals expect their communities to make full use of the very resources, courses, and personnel that they have fought for so persistently, equal attention must also be devoted to facilitating the maturation of Asian American students' racial identity.

Finally, an understanding of Asian American racial identity development may serve as a further reminder of the heterogeneity of the Asian American community. That is, Asian American students may differ in their responses to race and racial issues as well as in their identification with the Asian American community. As a result, the effectiveness of practitioners may be reflective of the extent to which the programs and events that they design are developmentally appropriate for the full range of racial identity statuses exhibited by the Asian American students on their respective campuses.

References

Alvarez, A. N., and Kimura, E. F. "Asian Americans and Racial Identity: Dealing with Racism and Snowballs." *Journal of Mental Health Counseling,* 2001, *23,* 192–206.

Alvarez, A. N., and Yeh, T. L. "Asian Americans in College: A Racial Identity Perspective." In D. Sandhu (ed.), *Asian and Pacific Islander Americans: Issues and Concerns for Counseling and Psychotherapy.* Huntington, N.Y.: Nova Science Publishers, 1999.

Ancheta, A. N. *Race, Rights, and the Asian American Experience.* New Brunswick, N.J.: Rutgers University Press, 1998.

Bagasao, P. Y. "Student Voices—Breaking the Silence: The Asian and Pacific American Experience." *Change,* Nov.-Dec. 1989, pp. 28–37.

Chun, K. T. "The Myth of Asian American Success and Its Educational Ramifications." *IRCD Bulletin,* 1980, *1 and 2,* 1–12. Reprinted in D. T. Nakanishi and T. Y. Nishida (eds.), *The Asian American Educational Experience: A Source Book for Teachers and Students.* New York: Routledge, 1995.

Cross, W. E., Jr. "The Negro-to-Black Conversion Experience: Toward a Psychology of Black Liberation." *Black World,* 1971, *20*(9), 13–27.

Cross, W. E., Jr. *Shades of Black.* Philadelphia: Temple University Press, 1991.

Espiritu, Y. L. *Asian American Panethnicity: Bridging Institutions and Identities.* Philadelphia: Temple University Press, 1992.

Evans, N. J., Forney, D. S., and Guido-DiBrito, F. *Student Development in College: Theory, Research, and Practice.* San Francisco: Jossey-Bass, 1998.

Helms, J. E. *Black and White Racial Identity: Theory, Research, and Practice.* Westport, Conn.: Greenwood Press, 1990.

Helms, J. E. "An Update of Helms's White and People of Color Racial Identity Models." In J. G. Ponterotto, J. M. Casas, L. A. Suzuki, and C. M. Alexander (eds.), *Handbook of Multicultural Counseling.* Thousand Oaks, Calif.: Sage, 1995.

Helms, J. E. "Model Minorities: Coping with Racism in Asian American Communities." Symposium conducted at the meeting of 108th Annual Convention of the American Psychological Association, Washington, D.C., Aug. 2000.

Helms, J. E., and Cook, D. A. *Using Race and Culture in Counseling and Psychotherapy: Theory and Process.* Needham Heights, Mass.: Allyn & Bacon, 1999.

Kohatsu, E. L. "The Effects of Racial Identity and Acculturation on Anxiety, Assertiveness, and Ascribed Identity Among Asian American College Students." Unpublished doctoral dissertation, University of Maryland, College Park, 1992.

Monaghan, P. "A New Momentum in Asian-American Studies." *Chronicle of Higher Education,* Apr. 2, 1999, pp. A16–A18.

Osajima, K. "The Hidden Injuries of Race." In L. A. Revilla, G. M. Nomura, S. Wong, and S. Hune (eds.), *Bearing Dreams, Shaping Visions.* Pullman: Washington State University Press, 1993.

Sanford, N. *Self and Society.* New York: Atherton Press, 1966.

Sue, D., Mak, W. S., and Sue, D. W. "Ethnic Identity." In L. C. Lee and N.W.S. Zane (eds.), *Handbook of Asian American Psychology.* Thousand Oaks, Calif.: Sage, 1998.

Suzuki, B. H. "Education and the Socialization of Asian Americans: A Revisionist Analysis of the 'Model Minority' Thesis." *Amerasia Journal,* 1977, *4*(2), 23–51. Reprinted in D. T. Nakanishi and T. Y. Nishida (eds.), *The Asian American Educational Experience: A Source Book for Teachers and Students.* New York: Routledge, 1995.

Uba, L. *Asian Americans: Personality Patterns, Identity, and Mental Health.* New York: Guilford, 1994.

Young, K., and Takeuchi, D. T. "Racism." In L. C. Lee and N.W.S. Zane (eds.), *Handbook of Asian American Psychology.* Thousand Oaks, Calif.: Sage, 1998.

ALVIN N. ALVAREZ *is assistant professor and coordinator of the college counseling program, Department of Counseling, San Francisco State University, San Francisco, California.*

5

Psychosocial student development theory based on predominantly white student populations may not be appropriate for Asian American students. The authors propose a new model of psychosocial development for Asian American students that takes racial identity and external influences into account.

An Asian American Perspective on Psychosocial Student Development Theory

Corinne Maekawa Kodama, Marylu K. McEwen, Christopher T. H. Liang, Sunny Lee

In recent years, discussion in higher education has centered on how practitioners can provide more effective and inclusive services for all students. Given that these services are often based on theoretical foundations that have been narrowly normed, it makes sense to examine some of these theories and their relevance to today's student populations. Arguments about developmental theories not reflecting the voices of women students (Belenky, Clinchy, Goldberger, and Tarule, 1986; Gilligan, 1982; Straub and Rodgers, 1986), African American students (McEwen, Roper, Bryant, and Langa, 1990), and gay and lesbian students (Levine and Evans, 1991) have been made. Similarly, we contend that the psychosocial development of Asian American students is not reflected adequately in the psychosocial theory of Chickering and Reisser (1993) and propose a model of psychosocial development that accounts more effectively for the experiences and development of Asian American students.

This model was developed from an examination of psychosocial themes and issues discovered in the research literature in combination with a critique of traditional student development theory, primarily Chickering's psychosocial student development theory (1969; Chickering and Reisser, 1993; for a more detailed critique, see Kodama, McEwen, Liang, and Lee, 2001). Although we are assuming some knowledge of Chickering's developmental model, a brief introduction to psychosocial theory and Chickering may be helpful.

NEW DIRECTIONS FOR STUDENT SERVICES, no. 97, Spring 2002 © Wiley Periodicals, Inc.

45

Psychosocial development, according to Parker, Widick, and Knefelkamp (1978), addresses "what students will be concerned about and what decisions will be primary" (p. xii). However, to date there has been no research examining psychosocial theory with Asian American students (Evans, Forney, and Guido-DiBrito, 1998).

Chickering's theoretical frame of student development (Chickering and Reisser, 1993) has been adopted widely and used by student affairs practitioners. In Chickering's model, developmental tasks are presented as seven core issues or challenges that the college student encounters: developing competency, managing emotions, moving through autonomy toward interdependence, developing mature interpersonal relationships, developing identity, developing purpose, and developing integrity. Chickering presents a typical pattern to the seven vectors, with the first four vectors providing the foundation for the fifth vector, which then leads to the final two vectors.

Most of the themes that emerged in this theoretical research as psychosocial issues for Asian American students mirrored the *content* areas of Chickering's seven vectors, though the specific *tasks* associated with those vectors, that is, *how* students negotiate or address those content areas, did not fit well. For example, emotions are an area of development that Asian American students are dealing with, but not necessarily learning how to "manage," as Chickering suggests. We frame our model in the context of two external domains that exert influences on Asian American students' development: Western values and racism from U.S. society and Asian values from family and community. How students are able to negotiate this tension of dominant societal norms and familial and cultural values influences the development of their identity.

External Influences and Domains

Life in the United States is dominated by Western values such as individualism, independence, and self-exploration, each of which underlies the development of traditional psychosocial theory. Another influence from dominant society is that of racism, which is often overlooked in terms of its influence on an individual's psychosocial development. Like many nonwhite groups in the United States, Asian Americans are often not exposed to the history of contributions and struggles of their own communities. Although their heritage is rendered invisible in education, their identity may have incorporated a variety of stereotypes from society and the media of who they are and what they should be. Hamamoto (1994) explains that these images serve to perpetuate "psychosocial dominance" (Baker, 1983, p. 35), as Asian Americans may begin to disdain their racial or ethnic background and even themselves. Essentially, "psychosocial dominance" refers to how racial minorities internalize racism and accept the primacy of Euro-American cultural values and social institutions (Espiritu, 1997). Identity, then, becomes a process of negotiating the mores of the dominant culture.

Racial identity, tied to the experience of all people of color with oppression (Helms, 1995), becomes central to a student's overall sense of identity and psychosocial development. Racial identity theories (Atkinson, Morten, and Sue, 1993; Helms, 1995), as Alvin Alvarez shows in Chapter Four, can help explain the various ways that students approach, negotiate, and understand their identity as racial beings and how it affects other aspects of their lives.

The second domain of influence on Asian American college students is traditional Asian familial and cultural values. These include the values of collectivism, interdependence, placing the needs of the family above the self, interpersonal harmony, and deference to authority, which often contradict those of the dominant Western society (Kim, Atkinson, and Yang, 1999). For example, Asian collectivism contrasts with Western individualism, which influences identity, as Western cultures view identity as the development of a self-actualized, autonomous individual, while Asian cultures view the identity of the individual as connected to the family unit (Huang, 1997). This presents a dilemma for Asian American students who are trying to negotiate and reconcile these conflicting influences with their own experiences at home and around peers.

Family and dominant white society may exert opposing forces on an Asian American student that both constrain and influence the student's development. However, some research indicates that Asian Americans are influenced strongly in their identity by others (Leong, 1985; Yeh and Huang, 1996), so external influences may have a greater impact on Asian American students than acknowledged in traditional theories, which portray identity development primarily as an individual process.

The degree of polarization between these two domains of familial and cultural values and dominant societal mores differs from student to student, based on generational status, level of acculturation, geographical location, peer groups, and proximity to Asian American political movements (Yeh and Huang, 1996). For instance, a first-generation Laotian American student whose family recently immigrated to the United States may experience more dissonance between Asian and Western values than a fourth-generation Chinese American student whose family has been in the United States since the early 1900s and has grown up with the dominant culture's values.

A Psychosocial Model for Asian American Students

In this new model of psychosocial development for Asian American students, we use much of the language of Chickering's theory, including ideas of competency, emotions, interdependence versus independence, identity, purpose, and integrity. However, we apply these terms to general content areas of development rather than associate them with specific tasks, and the order and emphasis on these areas differs from Chickering's original theory. A visual representation of this model is presented in Figure 5.1.

Figure 5.1. Asian Americans: Negotiating Identity and Developmental Tasks

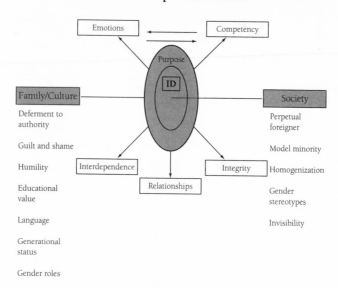

Central to the model is identity. Identity, according to Erikson (1968), embraces not only a sense of who one is as an individual but also a sense of self within one's family and community and some degree of congruence between one's view of oneself and others' views. Also central to this model is purpose, which includes vocational plans and aspirations as well as plans for college and the future.

In Figure 5.1, identity and purpose are represented as concentric circles, closely interrelated and as foundations for other areas of development. Since Asian Americans' pursuit of higher education is often pragmatic, goal-oriented, and job-related (Hune and Chan, 1997), purpose may be central to students' reasons for attending college as well as how they identify themselves. The interface between identity and purpose is semipermeable, suggesting that an Asian American college student's identity may be filtered through the student's educational and vocational purpose; purpose may even serve as a protection against developing identity. For example, for a student whose identity is defined primarily by personal career goals and family commitments, new experiences and points of view may have little influence in challenging the student's development around purpose or identity if they do not fit into this already established self-definition.

A change in identity for a student may result in a change of purpose (or vice versa) and may subsequently cause changes in other areas of development such as competency, emotions, interdependence, relationships, and integrity (visually portrayed as vectors, a term used by Chickering, 1969).

The circular pattern of these vectors represents their nonhierarchical and fluid nature, not assigning primacy to one over another.

This model of psychosocial development takes place in the context of external influences from dominant U.S. society and traditional Asian values from family. This is represented visually by an axis on which the student's development is situated, with the two domains located at either end. This representation shows that a student's development can shift toward one side or the other, depending on which domain is exerting a stronger influence at a particular time or on a particular issue. For some students, the distance between the two ends may be great, representing much incongruence between the dominant society and the values of their family. For others, the distance may be short, particularly if the student is relatively acculturated and feels little conflict between the domains of family and society.

Increased awareness of the relationship of self to the two domains promotes the development of identity and purpose, which in turn influences change and growth among the other five developmental tasks. This sense of empowerment can lead to greater self-efficacy, congruence, and holistic development. The further a student moves in her or his development, the better able the student is to negotiate the dissonance between the two domains.

Identity. Identity centers our model of understanding Asian American students' psychosocial development, as it involves development of an increasingly complex self. Identity development means that there is increasing congruence between one's own sense of self and external feedback (Erikson, 1968).

Developing a racial identity provides a foundation for Asian American students' overall identity development because of the primacy of racism on psychosocial development. Although Chickering and Reisser (1993) and other psychosocial theorists do not single out racial or ethnic identity in much detail, we find it crucially important for the identity development of Asian Americans. As Noel, a Pilipino American student, suggests, race "is such a key part of my identity . . . that to separate the racial or ethnic component from the rest of me would be to slice myself in half."

Asian American students face racism and stereotypes that may influence the way they see themselves. Asian Americans often report having encounters that create a sense of otherness—surprise at their fluent English speech, assumptions that they are not American, and stereotypes such as computer geek, martial arts expert, and exotic woman. Such incidents teach Asian Americans that people make assumptions about who they are based on their physical appearance, which may be incongruent with their own self-perceptions. Michelle, a Chinese-Japanese American, provides a good example of this contradiction: "I don't think I've ever seen myself as looking Asian, though other people do. I just thought I had a regular face. . . . It seemed weird to me that people make judgments about who I am just because of how I look. . . . Just because I look Asian or Asian American to others doesn't mean that I understand the Asian culture."

Identity issues may be even more complex for multiracial students of Asian descent, who face additional questions about their appearance, identity, and loyalties. They may experience conflicting messages about the importance of their racial and ethnic identities within their families, and they may question where they fit in due to the often mutually exclusive groupings of race and ethnic identification (King and DaCosta, 1996; Root, 1997). Multiracial students struggle not only with how others perceive them but also with how they view themselves and construct their identity.

Gender and sexual identity are often overlooked but are important to Asian American students' identity development in college. Gender identity is particularly salient for Asian American college-age women, who may be encountering peers or role models who have a more feminist point of view. This can be a dramatic identity issue if these new points of view conflict with family expectations and values (Bradshaw, 1994; Homma-True, 1997). Being gay or lesbian can be a complex identity issue for Asian Americans as people of color who are already dealing with an oppressive society (Wall and Washington, 1991). Coming-out issues for gay and lesbian Asian Americans may be especially difficult in a culture where sexuality is rarely talked about, much less homosexuality (Aoki, 1997; Chan, 1989, 1997; Huang, 1997; Leong, 1996). Further, being gay may be perceived as bringing shame to oneself and one's family, conflicting with Asian cultural values of family heritage, honor, and passing on the family name (Aoki, 1997; Chan, 1989).

Purpose. For many Asian Americans, purpose is often connected closely with the issue of academic achievement. To the extent that segments of the Asian American community subscribe to an academic- and economic-based definition of success, Asian Americans may decide early in their college career on a major that leads to a prestigious or high-paying job, resulting in respect and economic security for their family (Leung, Ivey, and Suzuki, 1994). Concerned about prestige and financial security, many Asian Americans study the sciences, engineering, health care fields, and business (Lee, 1996; Hune and Chan, 1997). However, for students who are not interested in these fields, family expectations may make it difficult to choose another major or career path. Thus it seems that Asian Americans may come to college with a clearer sense of purpose in terms of majors and careers but may be less likely to change that original goal despite shifts in academic and personal interests.

Another issue for Asian Americans related to purpose is developing an awareness and understanding of various career opportunities. Because of stereotyping, lack of role models, and an economic-based definition of success, Asian American students may not see the full range of options available for their future. A lack of Asian American role models may result in students not being able to envision themselves in particular careers, regardless of interest.

Interdependence affects purpose and career choice (Leong, 1995; Wong and Mock, 1997), as Asian Americans have expressed higher levels of dependent decision making (Leong and Gim-Chung, 1995). In fact, Leong (1995) found that Asian Americans were the only ethnic group to rank parental pressure as one of the five most influential reasons in career choice. Thus traditional career counseling, focusing primarily on exploration of individual interests, may not fit well. However, relevant tasks around purpose for Asian Americans might be developing an understanding of personal interests in terms of career and lifestyle, recognizing that one can change majors and career paths, reconciling individual interests with family expectations, and integrating career goals within the scope of a larger, more meaningful purpose.

Competency. Competency as developed by Chickering (1969; Chickering and Reisser, 1993) is a relevant developmental task for Asian American college students. However, for Asian American students, the focus seems to be on intellectual competency rather than the other types of competency (physical and manual, interpersonal) that Chickering highlights in his theory. This may relate to a cultural value on education (Hune and Chan, 1997; Wong and Mock, 1997), perceived by many Asian Americans not only as an economic necessity but also as a primary vehicle by which to achieve success in a racist society (Hune and Chan, 1997). Asian Americans may also internalize the myth of the "model minority" (see Chapter Three), whereby they are expected to do well intellectually. As a result, these students may experience "achievement stress" (Yamagata-Noji, 1987) as they place great pressure on themselves.

However, both interpersonal competency and physical competency may be challenges for Asian American students who have been taught to emphasize educational talents and goals (Wong and Mock, 1997). Social and interpersonal competency may be an even greater challenge for first-generation students, who may struggle with language barriers, cultural adjustments, or feelings of alienation, which contribute to a lack of confidence about their interpersonal abilities (Kiang, 1992).

Emotions. Asian cultural values include emotional discipline, inhibition of strong feelings, and use of restraint in interactions with others. Guilt and shame are often used as powerful controls (Lee, 1997; Liem, 1997; Uba, 1994) that affect how Asian Americans deal with emotions and behaviors. Further, there is some evidence that the long hours of hard work by Asian American parents (particularly recent immigrants) and a cultural tendency not to talk about discrimination and racism may result in neglect of children's emotional needs (Hong, 1993; Hongo, 1995; Lee, 1992).

Since withholding free expression of feelings is considered an important part of maintaining harmony (Chew and Ogi, 1987), Asian American college students may have had minimal modeling of emotional awareness and expression. Because the Asian cultural value places others' feelings above one's own (Wong and Mock, 1997), emotions may be an area of "untested waters" for many Asian American students. In a predominantly white college environment, however, expressiveness is often the norm, and Asian Americans may not be comfortable with others' openness (Chew and Ogi, 1987). Thus "exploring" or "understanding" emotions might be more appropriate tasks for Asian American students as they develop an awareness of a range of emotions, the appropriate expression of them, and which emotions are valued in a college environment (William Ming Liu, personal communication, Apr. 1998). This contrasts with Chickering's idea of "managing" emotions, which is based primarily on students' learning how to control "unruly" emotions (Chickering and Reisser, 1993, p. 83).

Interdependence Versus Independence. Interdependence is central to Asian cultures and families, with the Confucian values of filial piety and obligation to the family taking precedence over individual identity, wants, and desires (Lee, 1997). Western notions of adolescence as a time of separation and individuation (for example, separating psychologically and physically from parents) may consequently not fit the cultural values or life pattern of Asian Americans (Huang, 1997; Wong and Mock, 1997). Physical separation from Asian American parents often occurs only after marriage, and emotional separation, if it ever occurs, usually happens well into one's thirties rather than during the college years (Wong and Mock, 1997).

Family responsibility and support are central to interdependence for Asian Americans, particularly for students who serve as cultural brokers between their immigrant parents and the Western world. Asian American parents often exert strong parental guidance, particularly in terms of decisions to attend college (Choe, 1998) and career issues (Leong and Serafica, 1995). However, it is important to note that acculturation levels and generational statuses are influential variables in the development of autonomy and interdependence (Wong and Mock, 1997).

Asian Americans may need to learn how to see themselves as individuals outside their family group, which contrasts with students described by Chickering who are "looking out primarily for themselves" (Chickering and Reisser, 1993, p. 142) and focused on gaining independence and autonomy from their families. In a sense, Asian American students are moving through this area of development in a sort of reverse order from what is posited in Chickering's theory.

This interdependence with family may have a significant influence on students' social and emotional lives in college (Wong and Mock, 1997). Because of familial interdependence, Asian American students may be more likely to live at home than with peers (Yamagata-Noji, 1987) or attend college closer to home than move across the country (except to attend prestigious private schools). However, living at home or close to home can make it difficult for a student to become involved in the social life of the college and develop friendships or support networks outside the family.

Relationships. Maintaining harmonious interpersonal relationships is important in Asian cultures based on collectivism. Valued behaviors and personality traits include cooperation and accommodation, patience, humility, and nonconfrontation (Uba, 1994), along with respect for elders and deference to authority. As a result, relationships with family, peers, romantic partners, and authority figures may be different from one another, and so the development of interpersonal relationships can be quite complex.

A challenge for Asian American students is developing relationships with faculty and staff. Given the hierarchical nature of relationships and respect for elders in many Asian cultures, Asian American students may be more comfortable deferring to authority rather than approaching faculty to introduce themselves or ask questions. This affects classroom interactions, where verbal expression and interaction are valued and even necessary for evaluation purposes. This also has implications for Asian American students' relationships with student affairs staff, as Asian Americans may be more formal with their elders, more concerned about doing something wrong, and less likely to challenge an adviser's perspective. Thus an important task for Asian American students may be developing relationships with faculty and staff that may be culturally different from their relationships with elders within their families.

A significant variable to consider in Asian Americans' development of relationships is the demographics of the college environment, particularly if it is different from a student's home environment. For example, a student who grew up in a predominantly Asian American neighborhood may need to learn how to adjust to a white majority on campus, while students who grew up in predominantly white neighborhoods may be unaccustomed to seeing many other Asian Americans. Many students experience pressure to choose between Asian American and non–Asian American friends and frequently deal with issues of integration versus segregation (Choe, 1998; Lee, 1996).

Furthermore, developing quality relationships, both platonic and romantic, may become more complex as Asian American students address their racial identity and learn the impact of racism and racial identity on their relationships (Helms, 1995). Michelle provides an example of these challenges:

> I do face a milder form [of racism and discrimination] . . . ; I've gotten bad vibes from [my classmates]; they've been hesitant to make friends with me, though I've tried very hard . . . It's an awkward situation . . . I just go to class, sit by myself, get the most out of it that I can, and leave. It's just the fifty minutes I have to deal with them . . . I haven't really approached them . . . I feel very uncomfortable with it, as it's very awkward having people speculate . . . and look at you like you're an animal in a zoo.

An important relationship issue that occurs often in college for Asian American students is the dynamics around dating issues, particularly interracial dating (Mock, 1999; Wang, Sedlacek, and Westbrook, 1992). Stereotypes of Asian American women and men may influence perceptions by the opposite sex, both within and outside their own ethnic or racial group. In particular, dating between white men and Asian American women is common and often causes tension between Asian American men and women about community and racial identity. Interracial relationships can also give rise to family tension and conflicts related to identity, grandchildren, and carrying on the family name (Lee, 1997; Wong and Mock, 1997).

Integrity. For Asian Americans, integrity is determined within the context of one's family and community by how individuals represent their families, respect their ancestors, and uphold the family name. Thus Asian Americans may be negotiating integrity for self versus integrity of family. According to Chickering (Chickering and Reisser, 1993), increasing congruence between behavior and values and consistency in applying ethical principles are keys to developing integrity. Asian American students, because of the differences between traditional Asian values and those of the dominant society, may find it difficult to develop congruence in these ways. Thus learning how to maintain balance and congruence between these two often competing sets of cultural values is a likely challenge.

This idea of a contextual integrity contrasts with Chickering's discussion of "humanizing values" as the ability to "detach, to withhold judgment, while staying in touch with persistent feelings" (Chickering and Reisser, 1993, p. 243) and "personalizing values" as students find their own way and clarify values and principles of their own apart from those of peers, family, and society. Because emotional restraint is a value in many Asian cultures, being "in touch with one's feelings" may be challenging. Furthermore, because of the interdependent nature of Asian Americans, making a clear distinction between individual values and those of the family can be difficult. Thus Chickering's framework of understanding integrity may not be appropriate for use with Asian Americans, who may not be trying to separate their own values from others' values as much as to maintain a sense of self within the context of values from family and society.

Implications for Professional Practice

The model of psychosocial development presented in this chapter has been designed to broaden the perspective of the ways that students may develop throughout the college years. Despite growing diversity on today's campuses, student affairs professionals, in developing programs and services, tend to rely on traditional psychosocial theories based on assumptions that may not fit current student populations.

Student affairs professionals should consider the importance of racial identity development in working with Asian American students and how racial identity can affect other areas of development. A change in racial identity may alter how students see themselves, their relationships, and their purpose in life, resulting in a renegotiation of other aspects of development.

The centrality of identity and purpose, as well as the focus on academic and economic variables in defining success, is important to consider in Asian Americans' pursuit of higher education. The interrelationship between identity and purpose is also crucial: if identity and purpose are one and the same for highly career-path-focused individuals, perhaps deep reflection or a set of challenging experiences such as not doing well in one's major may be necessary for students to challenge their established identity and to develop an identity beyond that of a specific vocational focus.

An understanding of familial interdependence and expectations and their impact on decision making for Asian Americans may help reevaluate practice, particularly in academic advising, career counseling, and even leadership development. Traditional methods of focusing primarily on students' individual interests and desires may not be appropriate, and it is important to consider the role of family expectations and pressures as the student negotiates his or her future.

An awareness of Asian Americans' perspectives on emotions can help student affairs practitioners understand and work better with Asian American college students and perhaps identify some of the reasons for challenge in interpersonal settings. It is also a reminder that student affairs professionals cannot always rely on emotional cues to signal distress or difficulty and assume that the lack of emotional expression means that Asian American students are doing fine.

The impact of racism and the effect of cultural values should be considered in designing programming and services for Asian American students. Offering contextual experiences that address the impact of race and culture on student development increases Asian American students' ability to better navigate racism, understand clashing cultural values, and gain insight into why they may experience conflicts. The model minority stereotype is important to keep in mind because of its impact not only on educators' perceptions of Asian Americans but also on Asian American students themselves (Chun, 1995). Student affairs professionals should consider how challenged or burdened Asian American students are by this stereotype of success. Noel speaks about the effect of the model minority stereotype: "The model minority stereotype really bothers me . . . I think it makes people want to rebel against achieving more . . . because they're pigeonholed, they're told that you have to be a model minority . . . and that makes people want to rebel against that . . . and as a result against their racial identity."

In addition, providing and supporting Asian American studies programs, culturally and ethnically based student organizations, and a diverse student body, faculty, and staff help students understand their cultural heritage and learn from role models. Furthermore, these structures provide students with environments to explore the effects of the negotiation between familial and cultural influences and dominant cultural values on the students' sense of self and weaken the effects of psychosocial dominance. Angela, a Pilipina American, describes her experience: "I never knew our Asian American history. I knew about Pilipino history, but not about the contributions of Pilipinos here in America. I can finally see all the reasons for all those theories in my head about the way [we are] . . . This is talking about my grandfather or my dad . . . talking about my history, for once. I finally understood . . . why I felt the way I did growing up. I was really able to identify with the issues and with the people in class."

As a broader implication for theory and practice, the development of this new psychosocial model underscores the need to examine traditional theories critically in light of new and changing populations. It is important to look at the underlying assumptions of developmental theories that may be inapplicable to students from cultures with contrasting values. In the case of Chickering's theory, for example, the content areas of his theory make sense, but we challenge their specific meanings, associated tasks, and use in explaining Asian American students' development. In addition, descriptions that may seem to have negative connotations (for example, lack of experience with emotions and having an external locus of control) may not necessarily be negative in themselves but are perceived that way because of the Western biases inherent in student affairs professionals' understanding and application of a particular theory. Finally, external forces like racism and cultural values can greatly affect students' development, a perspective that contrasts with traditional views that development is an individual process. Thus it is not appropriate to continue to view diverse populations all through the same lens and rely on traditional theories to explain their development.

We suggest in this model of psychosocial student development that Asian American students will develop more fully as they understand themselves in the contexts of U.S. society, their families, and their communities. Understanding themselves in these contexts implies that parts of themselves are no longer silenced or denied, thereby enabling students to develop to their fullest potential. By creating more opportunities for students to explore themselves in college, socially imposed definitions of who and what is normal or developed are challenged. Knowing and taking into account students' familial and cultural contexts and helping them draw on their strengths and values, rather than viewing them as deficient in relation to dominant society ideals, will assist Asian American students in greater and more meaningful psychosocial development.

References

Aoki, B. K. "Gay and Lesbian Asian Americans in Psychotherapy." In E. Lee (ed.), *Working with Asian Americans: A Guide for Clinicians*. New York: Guilford, 1997.

Atkinson, D. R., Morten, G., and Sue, D. W. *Counseling American Minorities: A Cross-Cultural Perspective*. (4th ed.) Dubuque, Iowa: Brown/Benchmark, 1993.

Baker, D. G. *Race, Ethnicity, and Power: A Comparative Study*. London: Routledge & Kegan Paul, 1983.

Belenky, M. F., Clinchy, B. M., Goldberger, N. R., and Tarule, J. M. *Women's Ways of Knowing: The Development of Self, Voice, and Mind*. New York: Basic Books, 1986.

Bradshaw, C. "Asian and Asian American Women: Historical and political considerations in psychotherapy." In L. Comas Diaz and B. Greene (eds.), *Women of color: Integrating ethnic and gender identities in psychotherapy*. New York: Guilford, 1994.

Chan, C. S. "Issues of Identity Development Among Asian American Lesbians and Gay Men." *Journal of Counseling and Development*, 1989, *68*, 16–20.

Chan, C. S. "Don't Ask, Don't Tell, Don't Know: The Formation of a Homosexual Identity and Sexual Expression Among Asian American Lesbians." In B. Greene (ed.), *Ethnic and Cultural Diversity Among Lesbian and Gay Men*. Thousand Oaks, Calif.: Sage, 1997.

Chew, C. A., and Ogi, A. Y. "Asian American College Student Perspectives." In D. J. Wright (ed.), *Responding to the Needs of Today's Minority Students*. New Directions for Student Services, no. 38. San Francisco: Jossey-Bass, 1987.

Chickering, A. W. *Education and Identity*. San Francisco: Jossey-Bass, 1969.

Chickering, A. W., and Reisser, L. *Education and Identity*. (2nd ed.) San Francisco: Jossey-Bass, 1993.

Choe, Y. L. "Exploring the Experience of Asian Students at the University of Virginia." Unpublished paper, University of Virginia, 1998.

Chun, K. T. "The Myth of Asian American Success and Its Educational Ramifications." *IRCD Bulletin*, 1980, *1 and 2*, 1–12. Reprinted in D. T. Nakanishi and T. Y. Nishida (eds.), *The Asian American Educational Experience: A Source Book for Teachers and Students*. New York: Routledge, 1995.

Erikson, E. H. *Identity: Youth and Crisis*. New York: Norton, 1968.

Espiritu, Y. L. *Asian American Women and Men: Labor, Law, and Love*. Thousand Oaks, Calif.: Sage, 1997.

Evans, N. J., Forney, D. S., and Guido-DiBrito, F. *Student Development in College: Theory, Research, and Practice*. San Francisco: Jossey-Bass, 1998.

Gilligan, C. *In a Different Voice: Psychological Theory and Women's Development*. Cambridge, Mass.: Harvard University Press, 1982.

Hamamoto, D. Y. *Monitored Peril: Asian Americans and the Politics of TV Representation*. Minneapolis: University of Minnesota Press, 1994.

Helms, J. E. "An Update of Helms's White and People of Color Racial Identity Models." In J. G. Ponterotto, J. M. Casas, L. A. Suzuki, and C. M. Alexander (eds.), *Handbook of Multicultural Counseling*. Thousand Oaks, Calif.: Sage, 1995.

Homma-True, R. "Asian American Women." In E. Lee (ed.), *Working with Asian Americans: A Guide for Clinicians*. New York: Guilford, 1997.

Hong, M. (ed.). *Growing Up Asian American*. New York: Avon, 1993.

Hongo, G. (ed.). *Under Western Eyes: Personal Essays from Asian America*. New York: Anchor, 1995.

Huang, L. N. "Asian American Adolescents." In E. Lee (ed.), *Working with Asian Americans: A Guide for Clinicians*. New York: Guilford, 1997.

Hune, S., and Chan, K. S. "Special Focus: Asian Pacific American Demographic and Educational Trends." In D. J. Carter and R. Wilson (eds.), *Fifteenth Annual Status Report on Minorities in Higher Education, 1996–1997*. Washington, D.C.: American Council on Education, 1997.

Kiang, P. N. "Issues of Curriculum and Community for First-Generation Asian Americans in College." In L. S. Zwerling and H. B. London (eds.), *First-Generation Students: Confronting the Cultural Issues*. New Directions for Community Colleges, no. 80. San Francisco: Jossey-Bass, 1992.

Kim, B.S.K., Atkinson, D. R., and Yang, P. H. "The Asian Values Scale: Development, Factor Analysis, Validation, and Reliability." *Journal of Counseling Psychology*, 1999, *46*, 342–352.

King, R. C., and DaCosta, K. M. "Changing Face, Changing Race: The Remaking of Race in the Japanese American and African American Communities." In M.P.P. Root (ed.), *The Multiracial Experience.* Thousand Oaks, Calif.: Sage, 1996.

Kodama, C. M., McEwen, M. K., Liang, C.T.H., and Lee, S. "A Theoretical Examination of Psychosocial Issues for Asian Pacific American Students." *NASPA Journal,* 2001, *38,* 411–437.

Lee, E. "A Multicultural Coup at U-Md." *Washington Post,* Aug. 30, 2000, p. B1.

Lee, J.F.J. *Asian Americans: Oral Histories of First- to Fourth-Generation Americans from China, the Philippines, Japan, India, the Pacific Islands, Vietnam, and Cambodia.* New York: New Press, 1992.

Lee, S. J. *Unraveling the "Model Minority" Stereotype.* New York: Teachers College Press, 1996.

Leong, F.T.L. "Career Development of Asian Americans." *Journal of College Student Development,* 1985, *26,* 539–546.

Leong, F.T.L. (ed.). *Career Development and Vocational Behavior of Racial and Ethnic Minorities.* Mahwah, N.J.: Erlbaum, 1995.

Leong, F.T.L., and Gim-Chung, R. H. "Career Assessment and Intervention with Asian Americans." In F.T.L. Leong (ed.), *Career Development and Vocational Behavior of Racial and Ethnic Minorities.* Mahwah, N.J.: Erlbaum, 1995

Leong, F.T.L., and Serafica, F. C. "Career Development of Asian Americans: A Research Area in Need of a Good Theory." In F.T.L. Leong (ed.), *Career Development and Vocational Behavior of Racial and Ethnic Minorities.* Mahwah, N.J.: Erlbaum, 1995.

Leong, R. (ed.). *Asian American Sexualities: Dimensions of the Gay and Lesbian Experience.* New York: Routledge, 1996.

Leung, S. A., Ivey, D., and Suzuki, L. "Factors Affecting the Career Aspirations of Asian Americans." *Journal of Counseling and Development,* 1994, *72,* 404–410.

Levine, H., and Evans, N. J. "The Development of Gay, Lesbian, and Bisexual Identities." In N. J. Evans and V. A. Wall (eds.), *Beyond Tolerance: Gays, Lesbians, and Bisexuals on Campus.* Washington, D.C.: American College Personnel Association, 1991.

Liem, R. "Shame and Guilt Among First- and Second-Generation Asian Americans and European Americans." *Journal of Cross-Cultural Psychology,* 1997, *28,* 365–392.

McEwen, M. K., Roper, L. D., Bryant, D. R., and Langa, M. J. "Incorporating the Development of African-American Students into Psychosocial Theories of Student Development." *Journal of College Student Development,* 1990, *31,* 429–436.

Mock, T. A. "Asian American Dating: Important Factors in Partner Choice." *Cultural Diversity and Ethnic Minority Psychology,* 1999, *5,* 103–117.

Parker, C. A., Widick, C., and Knefelkamp, L. "Editors' Notes: Why Bother with Theory?" In L. Knefelkamp, C. Widick, and C. A. Parker (eds.), *Applying New Developmental Findings.* New Directions for Student Services, no. 4. San Francisco: Jossey-Bass, 1978.

Root, M.P.P. "Multiracial Asians: Models of Ethnic Identity." *Amerasia Journal,* 1997, *23*(1), 29–41.

Straub, C. A., and Rodgers, R. F. "An Exploration of Chickering's Theory and Women's Development." *Journal of College Student Development,* 1986, *27,* 216–224.

Uba, L. *Asian Americans: Personality Patterns, Identity, and Mental Health.* New York: Guilford, 1994.

Wall, V. A., and Washington, J. "Understanding Gay and Lesbian Students of Color." In N. J. Evans and V. A. Wall (eds.), *Beyond Tolerance: Gays, Lesbians, and Bisexuals on Campus.* Washington, D.C.: American College Personnel Association, 1991.

Wang, Y., Sedlacek, W. E., and Westbrook, F. D. "Asian Americans and Student Organizations: Attitudes and Participation." *Journal of College Student Development,* 1992, *33,* 214–221.

Wong, L., and Mock, M. R. "Asian American Young Adults." In E. Lee (ed.), *Working with Asian Americans: A Guide for Clinicians.* New York: Guilford, 1997.

Yamagata-Noji, A. "The Educational Achievement of Japanese-Americans." Unpublished doctoral dissertation. Claremont Graduate School, 1987.

Yeh, C. J., and Huang, K. "The Collectivistic Nature of Ethnic Identity Development Among Asian American College Students." *Adolescence*, 1996, *31*, 645–661.

Corinne Maekawa Kodama is assistant director, Office of Career Services, University of Illinois at Chicago.

Marylu K. McEwen is associate professor in college student personnel, Department of Counseling and Personnel Services, University of Maryland, College Park.

Christopher T. H. Liang is a doctoral student in counseling psychology and instructor in Asian American studies, University of Maryland, College Park.

Sunny Lee is assistant director, Cross-Cultural Center, University of California, Irvine.

6

Asian Americans are often thought of as high academic achievers. However, an overlooked and growing population of Asian American students are at risk educationally and may need additional programs and services to help them succeed in college.

Asian American College Students Who are Educationally at Risk

Theresa Ling Yeh

The concept of educational risk is generally not associated with Asian American students. Indeed, the tremendous growth in the number of Asian American students attending colleges and universities over the past decade obscures the fact that members of some Asian American ethnic groups have prospered in higher education while others have struggled to enter and remain in the educational system (Bennett and Debarros, 1998). For example, while 58.4 percent of Indian and Pakistani Americans have completed college, only 2.9 percent of Hmong Americans have college degrees (Ng, 1995). Numerous misinterpretations of similar data have led to the stereotyping of Asian Americans as a group of high-achieving students who possess the skills and knowledge needed to succeed at all levels of their education (Alva, 1993; Chun, 1995; Dao, 1991; Hu, 1989; Nakanishi, 1995; Siu, 1996; Suzuki, 1977, 1989). Unfortunately, for many Asian American students who are having academic difficulty, this perception of guaranteed educational success has proved detrimental because their needs have been systematically neglected at the institutional level.

Most studies on educationally at-risk students have focused on African American and Latino students or students at the elementary and secondary school level (Dao, 1991; Dolly, Blaine, and Power, 1989; Johnson, 1994; Presseisen, 1988; Rossi, 1994; Slavin, Karweit, and Madden, 1989). The retention of Asian American at-risk students at the postsecondary level is not regarded as an issue of concern, presumably due to the belief that postsecondary education goes beyond what is considered the basic level of education needed in the United States. Thus some researchers may operate on the premise that students in college have already "made it" and therefore do not need assistance. However, as college remediation and attrition rates continue to rise, higher education administrators must take the issue of student departure seriously, because universities have a responsibility to provide appropriate educational and personal support to students attending their institutions.

To address the disparity between the perception of Asian American educational success and the reality of students' unmet needs, this chapter seeks to integrate the research on educational risk with student departure theories as they pertain to Asian American college students. In addition, a central thesis of this chapter is that an invisible yet significant body of Asian American students exists who are struggling to complete high school and pursue higher education. Even more important, educators, counselors, and administrators at the secondary and postsecondary level need to develop a greater awareness of this population and make an effort to reach out and assist these students.

Defining Educational Risk

An "at-risk student" or "student at educational risk" has been defined as a student "with normal intelligence, whose academic background or prior performance may cause [her or him] to be perceived as a candidate for future academic failure or early withdrawal" (Educational Resources Information Center, 1987, p. 116). Traditional models of educational risk have taken an epidemiological approach, according to Johnson (1994), assuming that "students are at-risk by virtue of innate inadequacies and/or inadequacies that are the consequence of deprived, unhealthy homes" (p. 37). In contrast, Johnson proposes a more environmental approach that applies ecological theory to the concept of educational risk, arguing that students "are at-risk when they find themselves in environments for which they are ill-equipped" (p. 39). She describes a network of four systems, at the classroom, domestic, community, and sociocultural levels, and suggests that the interactions between a student and his or her environment are determined to be positive or detrimental based on the compatibility between the student's characteristics and the demands of the environment at each of these levels. Garcia, Wilkinson, and Ortiz (1995) later adapted this model, which was used subsequently by Siu (1996) in his discussion of factors that place Asian American students at risk. Similar to the systems just described, Siu grouped these risk factors into four categories pertinent to Asian American college students: individual, family, classroom and school, and community and society.

Risk Factors

Experts argue that educational risk cannot be predicted accurately by one variable alone and that the cumulative number of family stressors in one's life is related significantly to school dropout, whereas socioeconomic status alone is not (Frank, 1990). Theoretically, the more of these individual, family, school, and community risk factors that are present in a student's life, the less likely the student will be to pursue or complete higher education.

Individual Risk Factors. Individual risk factors are situations or characteristics that are "unique and inherent to the student" and therefore cannot be controlled by parents, faculty, or staff (Garcia, Wilkinson, and Ortiz, 1995, p. 448). While some of these factors may involve family members or external situations, they are still primarily personal traits that are distinct to each student.

Language. Numerous studies have indicated that English proficiency is one of the most reliable predictors of educational success (Cheng, 1995; Gordon, 1989; Ima and Rumbaut, 1989; Olsen and Chen, 1988; Trueba, Cheng, and Ima, 1993; Waggoner, 1991). Thus Asian American students who speak English as a second language may be at a disadvantage. Though educators may expect limited-English-proficient (LEP) college students to perform at the same level as native speakers, high school English courses rarely prepare these students to read and write with the skill that is sufficient for college-level work. Limited English-speaking ability can also hinder Asian American students' willingness to request support services, speak to professors, and socialize with classmates. These restrictions can often lead to a sense of helplessness and isolation and can contribute to higher rates of college attrition (Tinto, 1993).

Education. Siu (1996) indicates that immigrant students who have had more consistent schooling in their country of origin have a better chance of success than those whose education has been interrupted by war, resettlement, or other similar circumstances. This is because students with prior schooling are more familiar with the rules and expectations associated with a formal education system (for example, doing homework, taking tests) and are more likely to be literate in their native language, which can have a positive effect on their English acquisition skills when they move to the United States. Thus many Asian Americans, particularly refugees, are at a disadvantage because they did not receive an adequate, stable education in their country of origin.

Immigration Status. Studies have indicated that students who were born in foreign countries are twice as likely to be at risk as those who were born in the United States (Waggoner, 1991). The circumstances surrounding immigration can further affect educational persistence. For those who immigrate specifically for better educational opportunities, the motivation to complete a college degree is strong. However, the situation for refugees is considerably different, as these students often place less priority on higher education because they have more urgent stressors in their lives. Upon arrival in the United States, they must focus on caring for other family members, securing a job, and learning to speak English in order to survive. These refugees also face emotional trauma and psychological adjustment issues. Consequently, it is often difficult to recruit and retain Asian American students from these backgrounds (Uba, 1994).

Family Risk Factors. Overlapping considerably with individual risk factors, family risk factors involve a person's immediate or extended family, as well as the cultural expectations that the family subscribes to, and may be beyond the student's control.

Socioeconomic Status. Waggoner's study on undereducated Asian American youth (1991) found that those who fell below the poverty level were more than twice as likely to be at risk than those whose families were more affluent. Siu (1996) writes that "parents with economic survival needs have related stresses that make it hard for them to provide the supervision and support a student needs to succeed in school" (p. 20). Frequently, low family income results in the inability to pay for such expenses as application fees, tuition, textbooks, and transportation. In addition, financial hardship often means that low-income Asian American students must live at home, choose schools that are close and accessible by public transportation, and work extra hours to help support their families, all choices congruent with Asian cultural values of interdependence and obligation to family. These circumstances may make it difficult for students to concentrate on their studies and keep education as a top priority. For example, many low-income Asian American families are obligated to support extended family members or take care of younger siblings while the parents are working at two or three jobs. These financial obstacles can distract or prohibit low-income students from attending college, even when they are highly motivated.

Parents' Education. Kiang (1992) suggests that Asian American students who are the first in their families to attend college are at a disadvantage because of their parents' lack of experience with higher education. For students whose parents have little formal education, the perceived value of a college degree is often relatively low, reflecting their own perceived ability to attain a college degree (Astin, Astin, Bisconti, and Frankel, 1972; London, 1992; Nuñez and Cuccaro-Alamin, 1998; Trueba, Cheng, and Ima, 1993). In addition, parents with little educational background are often unable to assist their children with completing schoolwork, taking standardized tests, applying to college, and making career decisions. Thus for many first-generation students, unfamiliarity with the postsecondary educational process, coupled with their parents' inability to provide educational guidance, results in a low sense of academic self-confidence regarding acceptance to a college and completion of a bachelor's degree.

Family Support and Guidance. Related to first-generation and low-income status, family support and guidance with respect to higher education can vary greatly among Asian Americans. Asian parents who immigrate to the United States because they are specifically seeking better educational opportunities for their children will give their children unwavering emotional support. Among refugee students, however, parental support may not be as strong because these students are often expected to work full time immediately after high school or, in the case of young women, to get married and have children (Siu, 1996). There are also students whose parents are mentally or physically absent because they are working excessively long hours each day, were unable to accompany their children to the United States, or, in the case of wartime refugees, have posttraumatic emotional problems (Rumbaut, 1989). In these cases, family pressures and lack of support may force some Asian American students to choose between continuing their education and helping to take care of their families.

Institutional Risk Factors. Educational risk is also a function of a student's educational environment; thus institutional factors are those that are imposed by or directly related to the university or college the student is attending. These risk factors can also reflect the quality of the student's secondary school, as the two levels of education are directly related. Tinto (1993) suggests that the more a student feels socially and academically integrated into the college or university, the greater the likelihood of persistence through graduation, and vice versa. Similarly, Pascarella and Terenzini (1991) state that the quality and quantity of student contact with other people at the institution play a crucial role in college persistence.

Inadequate Academic Preparation. Undoubtedly, the quality of a student's academic preparation in high school affects the student's performance in college. Even though a student may graduate from high school and be admitted to a college or university, a lack of academic preparation can lead to either mandatory remediation or difficulty with college-level courses. For example, freshman remediation rates for the California state university system in fall 1999 indicated that at one university, 47 percent of Asian American and 61 percent of Pilipino American incoming freshmen were required to take remedial mathematics, and 58 percent and 46 percent, respectively, were required to take remedial English (California State University System, 2000).

Institutional Climate. Race and social class can be significant factors in student attrition, as students of color and students from low socioeconomic backgrounds often have more difficulty accessing the academic services and social support systems that are available to white students (Tinto, 1993). Thus students of color and students from low socioeconomic backgrounds may feel less integrated within the culture of predominantly white colleges. For Asian American LEP students, their limited English skills can often accentuate their "foreignness" and result in discrimination and hostility from others. Even on campuses with growing numbers of Asian American students, the climate can still reflect a negative atmosphere if faculty and staff promote the customs and values of traditionally white institutions. In fact, racially motivated violence and hate crimes continue to be directed toward Asian Americans at campuses across the country (Alvarez and Yeh, 1999; U.S. Commission on Civil Rights, 1992). These factors contribute to the institutional climate of a university and ultimately affect the retention of Asian American students.

Inadequate Institutional Support Programs. Although several models of support programs exist for at-risk students, many universities have not yet adopted them. And at colleges that do offer such programs, they are often underfunded, understaffed, and marginalized within the institution, making them unable to accommodate properly all the students who need their services. Furthermore, although career, advising, and counseling centers are ordinarily available to all students at a given institution, research suggests that Asian American students are less likely to use them (Sue and Sue, 1999; Uba, 1994). This underutilization can be attributed to a lack of knowledge about these resources, a reluctance to ask for help from unfamiliar adults, or a lack of staff who may be culturally sensitive to Asian American students.

Community and Societal Factors. Siu (1996) argues that "educational achievement does not take place in a vacuum, but in a community and societal context" (p. 29). These factors affect Asian Americans across ethnic and geographical lines because they can exist on a statewide, national, or even international level.

Model Minority Stereotype. A number of educators have discussed the negative effects of the model minority myth (see Chapter Three), which often invites resentment and hostility from members of the majority and other minority groups (Nakanishi, 1995; Suzuki, 1989). Specifically, the achievements of "successful" Asian Americans can mask the difficulties that at-risk students face. Thus many faculty and staff adopt the misconception that Asian Americans do not need support services. As a result of the model minority stereotype, Asian American students have often had to spend years petitioning for services and resources that have been available to African American and Chicano and Latino students for decades (Wei, 1993).

Intragroup Socioeconomic Gap. Unlike other minority groups, an unusually wide socioeconomic gap exists between Asian Americans of different ethnicities and immigration backgrounds (Omatsu, 1994). Often this polarization can be attributed to a family's immigration history. Historically, Asians from politically stable countries have been more academically successful, while those from impoverished, war-torn countries have not had the opportunity to focus on their education, thus limiting their career and income potential (Siu, 1996). For example, in 1990, some 42 percent of Cambodian families, 62 percent of Hmong families, and 32 percent of Laotian families fell below the federal income guidelines for poverty. Even within the same ethnic group, large gaps can exist between the wealthy and the poor, as is the case with the Chinese American population (Kwong, 1987). Especially in institutions with larger numbers of Asian Americans, affluent Asian American students rarely interact with those from lower socioeconomic backgrounds. This class division makes it difficult for those from disadvantaged backgrounds to advance educationally and economically because neither their institution nor their own communities provide them with support or assistance. Ultimately, this can lead to an even greater sense of isolation and marginality for at-risk Asian Americans in college.

Implications for Practice and Research

In working with Asian American students at educational risk, there are three main areas in which student affairs professionals can focus their efforts: recruitment, retention, and research.

Recruitment. Although many people would argue that Asian Americans do not need to be recruited because they already make up a high percentage of students at universities across the nation, it should be noted that most of the students they are referring to do not fall into the at-risk category. Instead, admissions and outreach counselors need to target Asian Americans from low-income, educationally disadvantaged backgrounds, rather than focus on race as a primary factor. More specifically, admissions officers can identify these students by reaching out to high schools in communities with large percentages of low-income Asian Americans, to community colleges, and to programs that serve low-income, first-generation students (for example, federal and state-funded programs such as TRIO and Educational Opportunity Programs). Frequently, Asian American students in these programs are highly motivated but may have apprehensions about attending four-year colleges, private colleges, or colleges that are farther away from home. Community colleges should also recruit educationally at-risk Asian Americans because these institutions can prepare these students to attend a four-year school or serve as an alternative to those who may not want to pursue a baccalaureate degree. Indeed, many Asian Americans attend community colleges to improve their English, save money, build their academic self-confidence, and make a more gradual transition to a four-year college.

In addition to recruiting at-risk Asian Americans to apply for admission, other student affairs staff can assist in outreach efforts. For example, residential life staff can encourage these students to apply for on-campus housing. Often Asian Americans from low-income, first-generation families are reluctant to live on campus, either because they believe the costs to be prohibitive or because their parents are afraid for the students to leave home. However, for many of these students, moving into the residence halls could be a positive developmental experience that enables them to meet people from other communities and also to concentrate on their academics without family stressors to distract them. For the many Asian American students who are unable or prefer not to live on campus for economic or cultural reasons, outreach needs to be conducted in order to assess their needs and provide appropriate services. In addition, in an effort to help demystify the financial aid process, financial aid officers could provide bilingual workshops to high school students and their parents. Such outreach staff can play a large role in dispelling myths about higher education and alleviating fears that these students may have about academic expectations, the cost of tuition, and general college survival. Involving parents may also be an important and culturally appropriate strategy in working with at-risk Asian Americans because of the strong influence parents will likely have on their children's educational plans.

Retention. Once at-risk Asian American students reach college, they need assistance in navigating the institution and maintaining good academic standing. Perhaps first and foremost, colleges and universities need to educate their faculty and staff about the existence of educationally at-risk Asian Americans within the institutions at which they work so that they can anticipate students' needs and suggest appropriate interventions.

As educators become more familiar with the needs of educationally at-risk Asian Americans, they can tailor student services to better serve these populations. Orientation offices and academic advising centers can recruit these students to attend special summer orientation and advising sessions to assist with course registration and other college procedures with which students and their parents and families may not be familiar. Learning or tutorial centers can target at-risk students by encouraging them to attend study skills workshops and use tutoring services. By providing training on the special needs and motivations of at-risk Asian American students, counseling and career center staff can more effectively serve this population. Asian American ethnic centers and student groups can also assist at-risk students by setting up peer mentoring programs and by building a sense of community among Asian American students across ethnic and socioeconomic lines. Finally, all offices can make an effort to hire multicultural and bilingual staff to work more closely with racially diverse and LEP students.

Some colleges and universities already have retention programs in place to serve students from low-income, first-generation backgrounds. For example, Educational Opportunity Programs (EOP) and Student Support Services (SSS) programs provide academic advising, career counseling, tutoring, and financial aid assistance from one central location. These programs often make it easier for students to seek help and also create a sense of community among the participants.

Research. In addition to the provision of direct services, more research on Asian American at-risk college students needs to be conducted. Whereas at-risk students from other racial and ethnic minority groups have been the subject of numerous studies, Asian Americans have been virtually ignored. The misperception that all Asian Americans are high academic achievers must be dispelled by research that demonstrates the existence of the low-income, first-generation subset of this population and highlights their needs and barriers to success. More specifically, research should focus on the academic and developmental issues that these students face and explore possible methods for coping with these issues. Once this population is recognized as being a viable group that is in need of support services, student affairs professionals can respond by creating more effective programs and services that will increase the personal development and retention of these students in higher education.

References

Alva, S. A. "Differential Patterns of Achievement Among Asian American Adolescents." *Journal of Youth and Adolescence,* 1993, *22,* 407–423.

Alvarez, A. N., and Yeh, T. L. "Asian Americans in College: A Racial Identity Perspective." In D. Sandhu (ed.), *Asian and Pacific Islander Americans: Issues and Concerns for Counseling and Psychotherapy.* Huntington, N.Y.: Nova Science Publishers, 1999.

Astin, H. S., Astin, A. W., Bisconti, A. S., and Frankel, H. H. *Higher Education and the Disadvantaged Student.* Washington, D.C.: Human Service Press, 1972.

Bennett, C. E., and Debarros, K. A. "The Asian and Pacific Islander Population." In U.S. Census Bureau, *The Official Statistics.* Washington, D.C.: U.S. Government Printing Office, 1998.

California State University System. "Fall 1999 Freshman Remediation Rates" [http://www.asd.calstate.edu/remrates99s], 2000.

Cheng, L. L. "Service Delivery to Asian-Pacific LEP Children: A Cross-Cultural Framework." In D. T. Nakanishi and T. Y. Nishida (eds.), *The Asian American Educational Experience: A Source Book for Teachers and Students.* New York: Routledge, 1995.

Chun, K. T. "The Myth of Asian American Success and Its Educational Ramifications." *IRCD Bulletin,* 1980, *1* and *2,* 1–12. Reprinted in D. T. Nakanishi and T. Y. Nishida (eds.), *The Asian American Educational Experience: A Source Book for Teachers and Students.* New York: Routledge, 1995.

Dao, M. "Designing Assessment Procedures for Educationally At-Risk South Asian American Students." *Journal of Learning Disabilities,* 1991, *24,* 594–601, 629.

Dolly, J. P., Blaine, D. D., and Power, K. M. "Educationally At-Risk Pacific and Asian Students in a Traditional Academic Program." *Journal of Instructional Psychology,* 1989, *16,* 155–163.

Educational Resources Information Center (ERIC). *Thesaurus of ERIC Descriptors.* Phoenix, Ariz.: Oryx, 1987.

Frank, J. R. "High School Dropouts: A New Look at Family Variables." *Social Work in Education,* 1990, *13*(1), 34–47.

Garcia, S. B., Wilkinson, C. Y., and Ortiz, A. A. "Enhancing Achievement for Language Minority Students: Classroom, School, and Family Contexts." *Education and Urban Society,* 1995, *27,* 441–462.

Gordon, L. W. "National Surveys of Southeast Asian Refugees: Methods, Findings, Issues." In D. W. Haines (ed.), *Refugees as Immigrants: Cambodians, Laotians, and Vietnamese in America.* Lanham, Md.: Rowman & Littlefield, 1989.

Hu, A. "Asian Americans: Model Minority or Double Minority?" *Amerasia Journal,* 1989, *15,* 243–257.

Ima, K., and Rumbaut, R. G. "Southeast Asian Refugees in American Schools: A Comparison of Fluent-English-Proficient and Limited-English-Proficient Students." In D. T. Nakanishi and T. Y. Nishida (eds.), *The Asian American Educational Experience: A Source Book for Teachers and Students.* New York: Routledge, 1995.

Johnson, G. M. "An Ecological Framework for Conceptualizing Educational Risk." *Urban Education,* 1994, *29,* 34–49.

Kiang, P. N. "Issues of Curriculum and Community for First-Generation Asian Americans in College." In L. S. Zwerling and H. B. London (eds.), *First-Generation Students: Confronting the Cultural Issues.* New Directions for Community Colleges, no. 80. San Francisco: Jossey-Bass, 1992.

Kwong, P. *The New Chinatown.* New York: Hill & Wang, 1987.

London, H. B. "Transformations: Cultural Challenges Faced by First-Generation Students." In L. S. Zwerling and H. B. London (eds.), *First-Generation Students: Confronting the Cultural Issues.* New Directions for Community Colleges, no. 80. San Francisco: Jossey-Bass, 1992.

Nakanishi, D. T. "Growth and Diversity: The Education of Asian-Pacific Americans." In D. T. Nakanishi and T. Y. Nishida (eds.), *The Asian American Educational Experience: A Source Book for Teachers and Students.* New York: Routledge, 1995.

Ng, F. (ed.). *The Asian American Encyclopedia.* New York: Marshall Cavendish, 1995.

Nuñez, A.M., and Cuccaro-Alamin, S. *First-Generation Students: Undergraduates Whose Parents Never Enrolled in Postsecondary Education.* Washington D.C.: Office of Educational Research and Improvement, 1998.

Olsen, L., and Chen, M. T. *Crossing the Schoolhouse Border: Immigrant Students and the California Public Schools.* San Francisco: California Tomorrow, 1988.

Omatsu, G. "The 'Four Prisons' and the Movements of Liberation: Asian American Activism from the 1960s to the 1990s." In K. Aguilar–San Juan (ed.), *The State of Asian America: Activism and Resistance in the 1990s.* Boston: South End Press, 1994.

Pascarella, E. T., and Terenzini, P. T. *How College Affects Students.* San Francisco: Jossey-Bass, 1991.

Presseisen, B. Z. "Teaching Thinking and At-Risk Students: Defining a Population." In B. Z. Presseisen (ed.), *At-Risk Students and Thinking: Perspectives from Research.* Washington D.C.: National Education Association of the United States and Research for Better Schools, 1988.

Rossi, R. J. (ed.). *Schools and Students at Risk: Context and Framework for Positive Change.* New York: Teachers College Press, 1994.

Rumbaut, R. G. "Portraits, Patterns, and Predictors of the Refugee Adaptation Process: Results and Reflections from the IHARP Panel Study." In D. W. Haines (ed.), *Refugees as Immigrants: Cambodians, Laotians, and Vietnamese in America.* Lanham, Md.: Rowman & Littlefield, 1989.

Siu, S. F. *Asian American Students at Risk: A Literature Review.* Baltimore: Center for Research on the Education of Students Placed at Risk, Johns Hopkins University, 1996. (ED 404 406)

Slavin, R. E., Karweit, N. L., and Madden, N. A. *Effective Programs for Students at Risk.* Needham Heights, Mass.: Allyn & Bacon, 1989.

Sue, D. W., and Sue, D. *Counseling the Culturally Different: Theory and Practice.* (3rd ed.) New York: Wiley, 1999.

Suzuki, B. H. "Education and the Socialization of Asian Americans: A Revisionist Analysis of the 'Model Minority' Thesis." *Amerasia Journal,* 1977, 4(2), 23–51. Reprinted in D. T. Nakanishi and T. Y. Nishida (eds.), *The Asian American Educational Experience: A Source Book for Teachers and Students.* New York: Routledge, 1995.

Suzuki, B. H. "Asian Americans as the 'Model Minority': Outdoing Whites? Or Media Hype?" *Change,* Nov.-Dec. 1989, pp. 13–19.

Tinto, V. *Leaving College: Rethinking the Causes and Cures of Student Attrition.* (2nd ed.) Chicago: University of Chicago Press, 1993.

Trueba, H. T., Cheng, L.R.L., and Ima, K. *Myth or Reality? Adaptive Strategies of Asian Americans in California.* Washington, D.C: Falmer Press, 1993.

Uba, L. *Asian Americans: Personality Patterns, Identity, and Mental Health.* New York: Guilford, 1994.

U.S. Commission on Civil Rights. *Civil Rights Issues Facing Asian Americans in the 1990s.* Washington D.C.: U.S. Commission on Civil Rights, 1992.

Waggoner, D. *Undereducation in America: The Demography of High School Dropouts.* Westport, Conn.: Auburn House, 1991.

Wei, W. *The Asian American Movement. Philadelphia:* Temple University Press, 1993.

THERESA LING YEH is assistant director of the Upward Bound program at the Haas Center for Public Service, Stanford University, Palo Alto, California.

7

Collaborations between student affairs professionals and Asian American studies faculty may be mutually beneficial by contributing to holistic student development and creating supportive environments for Asian American students.

Student Affairs and Asian American Studies: An Integrative Perspective

Alvin N. Alvarez, William Ming Liu

The increase in the number of Asian American students in higher education (Monaghan, 1999; U.S. Department of Education, 1999) has been paralleled by an expansion of Asian American studies (AAS) as an academic discipline. The growth of the Asian American student body, coupled with a politicized consciousness about race, gender, and class, has led to renewed interest in establishing AAS at universities across the nation (Monaghan, 1999). Indeed, collaboration among students, student affairs professionals, faculty, and community advocates has been central to the success of establishing AAS courses and programs at such universities as Northwestern (Garza, 1995), Princeton ("Princeton Students," 1995), Columbia (Yip, 1996), the University of California–Irvine (Lindgren, 1993; Tran and Laitt, 1993), and the University of Maryland, College Park (Lee, 2000). However, to capitalize on this success, continued collaboration between academic and applied disciplines will be crucial in the ongoing development and implementation of Asian American studies.

Thus the goal of this chapter is to outline a rationale for a continuing dialogue between student affairs and AAS. A central assumption of this chapter is that an integration of student affairs as an applied profession with Asian American studies as an academic discipline can assist all students, but in particular Asian Americans, in integrating their intellectual growth with their psychosocial development. Assuming that readers are somewhat familiar with student affairs history and literature, this chapter begins with a brief overview of AAS, followed by a general exploration of collaboration points between AAS and student affairs. The authors address two main questions in exploring the integration of the two fields: "What can AAS offer student affairs?" and "What can student affairs offer AAS?"

NEW DIRECTIONS FOR STUDENT SERVICES, no. 97, Spring 2002   © Wiley Periodicals, Inc.

What Is Asian American Studies?

AAS emerged in the late 1960s (Chan, 1991; Hune, 1995; Wei, 1993). Dissatisfied students of color advocated for courses that were both relevant and reflective of their experiences and their communities (Nakanishi, 1995–1996). Students demanded a curriculum that "included an incisive analysis of the history of racism, sexism, and class oppression in the United States; an accurate portrayal of the contributions and struggles of people of color; and practical training to enable graduates to bring about fundamental social change in their ethnic communities as well as in society at large" (Chan, 1991, p. 181). Distinct from Asian studies, Asian American studies focused on the culture and experiences of the Asian diaspora, Asians in America, and the process of racialization that transformed their ethnic differences into a unified racial group. Central to AAS was the examination of Asian Americans' experiences with racism, exclusion, and cultural transformations.

Although AAS programs initially incorporated community advocacy and participation in the curriculum, as social conditions slowly changed, AAS was charged with being less focused on the community as it developed into a traditional academic discipline throughout the 1980s (Omi and Takagi, 1995). That is, AAS had become a field where theory seemed to override community development and participation (Hirabayashi, 1998; Omi and Takagi, 1995) as issues of tenure, publications, and institutional prestige took precedence over student and community involvement. Responding to these criticisms, some AAS academics have sought not only to redefine AAS and its ties with the community but also to reemphasize community development as a core tenet (Hirabayashi, 1998; Osajima, 1998). Just as AAS redefines its relationships with the community, an impetus for this chapter is the need to examine the benefits of continued collaboration between Asian American studies and student affairs as it relates to the educational experiences of Asian American students. As a first step, both student affairs professionals and Asian American studies faculty need to clearly understand and articulate the strengths and expertise that they each bring to this collaboration.

What Can Asian American Studies Offer Student Affairs?

Being well informed about Asian American community issues (for example, discrimination, immigration) is necessary if one is to advocate for Asian American students. Often Asian American students who feel alienated from their campus seek out other Asian and Asian American faculty and staff to create community and ease their sense of marginalization (Lunneborg and Lunneborg, 1985). However, being an Asian or Asian American faculty or staff member does not qualify one to be an effective advocate. Sometimes students are unaware that an "Asian American" consciousness is a developed sensibility, not an inherited one. Unfortunately, Asian American faculty and administrators and others who may have empathy and an understanding of students' issues often are absent from institutions of higher education (Saigo, 1999). Hence one of the contributions of AAS programs may be to increase the number of and access to faculty, administrators, and staff who are cognizant of Asian American issues and concerns.

AAS can also help student affairs better contextualize advocacy efforts. As students and staff advocate for Asian American issues on their respective campuses, it is critical to understand that the inequities they perceive may be part of systemic patterns of both neglect and oppression directed at Asian Americans. With an awareness of the historical and sociopolitical context of their work, student affairs professionals may need to reevaluate their work with Asian American students. For instance, programming of only dances, cultural shows, and food fairs without an equal emphasis on understanding a larger sociopolitical context may be insufficient in promoting Asian American student development within a larger racialized context. That is, dances and cultural shows tend to be aesthetic rather than pedagogical partly because these activities become ritualized events rather than activities that build on students' development. Consequently, professionals may need to reassess their programming goals with respect to issues of race and question if Asian American student needs are met fully.

Contextualization is integral to the defense of Asian American students' advocacy goals. While a sense of social injustice may be the initial impetus for student advocacy, articulating one's understanding of both sociopolitical context and historical precedents is critical for an effective advocate. Particularly in an academic environment of fiscal accountability, student affairs professionals and students need to respond to the skeptical questions of administrators, academic senates, and faculty members with substantive arguments (Blimling, 1999) and clearly articulated rationales rather than plaintive anecdotes about the needs of the Asian American student community. Typical questions that require cogent responses are "What is the difference between Asian and Asian American studies?" "Is such a program really necessary, or can it be covered in other courses?" "Does every single community need a course about itself?" and "Why is it necessary to hire a dean, a psychologist, a program coordinator, or the like for Asian American students?" If student affairs professionals and student activists expect to answer such questions effectively, an understanding of Asian American history and sociopolitical contexts is integral to an effective response.

AAS also has the potential to broaden student affairs' conceptualization of both community and change. Typically, advocacy efforts on issues such as curriculum, staff visibility, retention, admissions, and student support services are focused at one university or college. However, a strength of disciplines such as Asian American studies and ethnic studies lies in their potential to expose students and student affairs professionals to the need for change at a more global level, beyond the confines of a particular university, student population, or racial group. Consequently, students may develop an awareness of issues beyond academia, such as immigration, legislation, housing, and employment, as well as an awareness of the shared struggles of Asian Americans and other oppressed groups (for example, African Americans, Latinos, and gays and lesbians). Insofar as student affairs professionals strive to instill in their students a sense of social justice that generalizes to students' postcollegiate lives, the lessons learned from AAS will be critical in exposing students to the many inequities beyond the walls of academia.

In light of the complementary goals of both professions, collaboration between AAS and student affairs seems to provide a natural link between the theoretical and the applied, the intellectual and the psychosocial, and the historical and the present. Kuh (1996) argued that such collaborations create a "seamless learning environment." For instance, class lectures on Asian ethnoviolence can be accentuated by involving students in a service-learning project designed to educate Asian American communities about ethnoviolence and local social and legal services. Similarly, in addition to learning about Asian American political empowerment through case studies on individuals such as Congressman Dalip Singh Saund, the first Asian American member of Congress (Fong, 1998), students can experience the process of political empowerment firsthand by participating in activities designed to increase Asian American student representation on campus governing bodies.

Increased collaboration between AAS and student affairs may serve as a model for integrating the learning experiences of students. Yet to reform undergraduate education (Schroeder, 1999), partnerships between academic units and student affairs require "a whole new mindset . . . to capitalize on the interrelatedness of the in- and out-of-class influences on student learning and the functional interconnectedness of academic and student affairs divisions" (Terenzini and Pascarella, 1994, p. 32). However, for a partnership between student affairs and AAS to be effective, both professions need to reassess and challenge their assumptions about what constitutes "learning," where "learning" occurs, and ultimately who can be described as an "educator."

What Can Student Affairs Offer Asian American Studies?

Sometimes it seems that AAS and student affairs collaborate only on the initial tasks involved in creating a AAS program. However, after a program is established, do practitioners and AAS faculty separate into their respective traditional roles? How do we conceptualize and program for student development once an AAS program has been established? What role can student affairs play in the implementation of such a program? How can student affairs be integrated into existing AAS programs?

One answer to these questions, for those in the initial stages of establishing AAS, is to integrate student affairs into AAS from the onset. First, AAS may include courses taught by student affairs professionals that reflect their knowledge and skills in areas such as leadership theory, student development, and educational issues and policy. In the classroom, student affairs professionals can enhance faculty's instructional effectiveness by coteaching and contributing their understanding of active learning techniques, experiential exercises, and individual and group processing skills. These competences are especially important, for AAS courses are often emotionally evocative. Second, AAS faculty and student affairs professionals can work collaboratively to look for community service experiences. Examples of such partnerships could be with community centers, government agencies, and nonprofit community agencies that serve Asian Americans. Finally, Asian American students need to be aware that establishing an AAS program is only one step in creating a multicultural community and that they should be vigilant in developing relationships with other "marginalized" communities (for example, groups for African Americans; lesbian, gay, bisexual, and transgender individuals; and Latinos).

For student affairs professionals on campuses with established AAS programs, developing relationships is partly a matter of knowing what student affairs can offer. Student affairs professionals need to recognize and articulate the value of student development theory as it relates to AAS. Racial identity theory (Helms, 1995), cognitive development theory (Perry, [1970] 1999), and gay and lesbian identity theory (D'Augelli, 1994), and others may be useful in helping AAS faculty appreciate the full range of developmental changes and reactions elicited by their courses. Similarly, an awareness of the developmental implications of their work may be a catalyst for AAS faculty to reevaluate curriculum and course design.

With a theoretical emphasis on developmental models of growth and a recognition of the concept of "challenge and support" (Sanford, 1966), student affairs professionals are well equipped to help AAS faculty in designing courses, lectures, and activities that are developmentally appropriate for students. For example, an understanding of the process of change involved in racial identity development may enable AAS faculty to develop a sequence of courses or lectures designed to facilitate students' movement from racial naiveté to racial awareness (Helms, 1995). Both lectures and activities may be tailored with greater sensitivity to specific developmental "challenges" that students face. For instance, films addressing a historical overview of Asian American immigration may be more developmentally appropriate for students early in racial identity development than a provocative film on anti-Asian ethnoviolence and harassment. Thus to the extent that student affairs can help AAS faculty link course material to the developmental needs of the students, one may discover that developmental considerations may become as central to the goals of AAS courses as the retention and analysis of facts and concepts.

With an understanding of student development theory (Evans, Forney, and Guido-DiBrito, 1998), student affairs professionals can broaden both students' and faculty's conceptualization of change. Despite seemingly disparate historical and philosophical foundations, the goal of initiating and facilitating change on varying dimensions (individual, social, and political) is common to both AAS and student affairs. Whereas AAS often focuses on examining and initiating change at a macro level—that is, sociologically and historically—a strength of student affairs is its understanding of change at a micro level, specifically intrapsychic and psychosocial development (Evans, Forney, and DiBrito, 1998). Hence to collaborate effectively, both professions need to teach their students about the necessity for change at both the macro and micro levels.

Beyond the theoretical and conceptual contributions of student affairs, the applied skills of student affairs practitioners are especially valuable to AAS faculty. A central focus of student affairs training as an applied profession is to provide professionals with both the skills and the criteria for competent and ethical service delivery (McEwen and Talbot, 1998). As an academic discipline in which community is one main focus of study, AAS may benefit from the expertise of an applied profession whose training focuses on service delivery to communities. For instance, because community service is integral to an AAS program, student affairs professionals may contribute to service learning projects by assisting in the program's design and implementation, acting as supervisors, and contributing their understanding of group and organizational dynamics. Thus student affairs professionals may be instrumental in bringing to life much of what is taught in Asian American studies courses.

Conclusion

Adopting an integrative perspective on student affairs and AAS involves a challenge to rethink service delivery as it relates to the educational and developmental needs of Asian American students. Continuing to allocate educational and professional services based on a dualistic conceptualization of student needs (that is, intellectual versus psychosocial) and student experiences (that is, in-class versus out-of-class experiences) disregards the complexity of student development and underestimates the potential of "education." Perhaps educators, both staff and faculty alike, would do well to remember that the ultimate criterion for educational success is reflected in the development of the student as a whole individual, spanning multiple and interdependent domains of growth (for example, Kezar and Moriarty, 2000). Insofar as student affairs professionals and Asian American studies faculty agree with such a criterion, an ongoing discourse between these professionals is crucial in forging an integration of disciplines designed to enhance the educational experiences of Asian American students.

References

Blimling, G. S. "Accountability in Student Affairs: Trends for the 21st Century." In C. S. Johnson and H. E. Cheatham (eds.), *Higher Education Trends for the Next Century.* Washington, D.C.: American College Personnel Association, 1999.

Chan, S. *Asian Americans: An Interpretive History.* Boston: Twayne, 1991.

D'Augelli, A. R. "Identity Development and Sexual Orientation: Toward a Model of Lesbian, Gay, and Bisexual Development." In E. J. Trickett, R. J. Watts, and D. Birman (eds.), *Human Diversity: Perspectives on People in Context.* San Francisco: Jossey-Bass, 1994.

Evans, N. J., Forney, D. S., and Guido-DiBrito, F. *Student Development in College: Theory, Research, and Practice.* San Francisco: Jossey-Bass, 1998.

Fong, T. P. *The Contemporary Asian American Experience: Beyond the Model Minority.* Upper Saddle River, N.J.: Prentice Hall, 1998.

Garza, M. "Asian Students at NU Continue Fasting for New Program." *Chicago Tribune,* Apr. 17, 1995, p. 2C3.

Helms, J. E. "An Update of Helms's White and People of Color Racial Identity Models." In J. G. Ponterotto, J. M. Casas, L. A. Suzuki, and C. M. Alexander (eds.), *Handbook of Multicultural Counseling.* Thousand Oaks, Calif.: Sage, 1995.

Hirabayashi, L. R. "Introduction." In L. R. Hirabayashi (ed.), *Teaching Asian America: Diversity and the Problem of Community.* Lanham, Md.: Rowman & Littlefield, 1998.

Hune, S. "Opening the American Mind and Body: The Role of Asian American Studies." In D. T. Nakanishi and T. Y. Nishida (eds.), *The Asian American Educational Experience: A Source Book for Teachers and Students.* New York: Routledge, 1995.

Kezar, A., and Moriarty, D. "Expanding Our Understanding of Student Leadership Development: A Study Exploring Gender and Ethnic Identity." *Journal of College Student Development,* 2000, *41,* 55–69.

Kuh, G. D. "Guiding Principles for Seamless Learning Environments for Undergraduates." *Journal of College Student Development,* 1996, *37,* 135–148.

Lee, E. "A Multicultural Coup at U-Md." *Washington Post,* Aug. 30, 2000, p. B1.

Lindgren, K. "UC Irvine: Asian American Studies Demanded." *Los Angeles Times,* Apr. 22, 1993, p. A3.

Lunneborg, P. W., and Lunneborg, C. E. "Student-Centered Versus University-Centered Solutions to Problems of Minority Students." *Journal of College Student Personnel,* 1985, *26,* 224–228.

McEwen, M. K., and Talbot, D. M. "Designing the Student Affairs Curriculum." In N. J. Evans and C. E. Phelps Tobin (eds.), *The State of the Art of Preparation and Practice in Student Affairs.* Lanham, Md.: University Press, 1998.

Monaghan, P. "A New Momentum in Asian-American Studies." *Chronicle of Higher Education,* Apr. 2, 1999, pp. A16–A18.

Nakanishi, D. T. "Linkages and Boundaries: Twenty-Five Years of Asian American Studies." *Amerasia Journal,* 1995–1996, *21*(3), xvii–xxv.

Omi, M., and Takagi, D. "Thinking Theory in Asian American Studies." *Amerasia Journal,* 1995, *21*(1–2), xi–xv.

Osajima, K. "Pedagogical Considerations in Asian American Studies." *Journal of Asian American Studies,* 1998, *1,* 269–292.

Perry, W. G., Jr. *Forms of Intellectual and Ethical Development in the College Years: A Scheme.* San Francisco: Jossey Bass, 1999. (Originally published 1970)

"Princeton Students Protest for Ethnic Studies." *Chronicle of Higher Education,* May 5, 1995, p. A4.

Saigo, R. H. "Academe Needs More Leaders of Asian-Pacific Heritage." *Chronicle of Higher Education,* Apr. 23, 1999, p. A72.

Sanford, N. *Self and Society.* New York: Atherton Press, 1966.

Schroeder, C. C. "Partnerships: An Imperative for Enhancing Student Learning and Institutional Effectiveness." In J. H. Schuh and E. H. Whitt (eds.), *Creating Successful Partnerships Between Academic and Student Affairs.* New Directions for Student Services, no. 87. San Francisco: Jossey-Bass, 1999.

Terenzini, P. T., and Pascarella, E. T. "Living with Myths: Undergraduate Education in America." *Change,* Jan.-Feb. 1994, pp. 28–32.

Tran, D., and Laitt, M. "UC Irvine Protest Ends in Accord on Asian American Studies Program." *Los Angeles Times,* June 11, 1993, p. B8.

U.S. Department of Education. *Digest of Education Statistics, 1999.* Washington, D.C.: U.S. Government Printing Office, 1999.

Wei, W. *The Asian American Movement.* Philadelphia: Temple University Press, 1993.

Yip, A. "APAs Fight for AAS: Fighting for Their Right." *Asian Week,* June 12–18, 1996, p. 14.

ALVIN N. ALVAREZ is assistant professor and coordinator of the college counseling program, Department of Counseling, San Francisco State University, San Francisco, California.

WILLIAM MING LIU is assistant professor of counseling psychology, University of Iowa, Iowa City.

8

Cultural factors can influence the way Asian American students display leadership as well as how they are perceived as leaders. Redefining leadership and devising inclusive leadership development programs can help to empower Asian American students and encourage them to become more involved on campus.

Developing Asian American Leaders

Christopher T. H. Liang, Sunny Lee, Marie P. Ting

Though Asian Americans have played an integral part in institutional change in higher education since the 1960s (Wei, 1993), the understanding of leadership and activism for this population is limited. In fact, Yammarino and Jung (1998) found only four articles that discussed leadership as it pertains to Asian Americans. One reason for this lack of understanding of Asian Americans may be a result of this population's being stereotyped as passive, unassertive, docile, and therefore lacking leadership skills. Goto (1999) explains that another reason is how leadership has been traditionally viewed and how it continues to be narrowly defined. Yammarino and Jung explain that our current understanding of leadership skills excludes practices generally found among Asian Americans, such as subordination of the individual to the group, deference, and obedience to elders. Further, Liu and Sedlacek (1998) argue that the definition of leadership should be expanded so that Asian Americans engaged in activities with their communities see themselves as leaders, easing their transition into broader leadership roles. The purpose of this chapter is to discuss cultural values that may affect how Asian Americans display leadership, address how race and racism may influence involvement and leadership, and describe three leadership development programs for Asian American students. Through this discussion we hope to broaden the understanding of Asian Americans and the definition of leadership and leadership development.

In understanding leadership among Asian Americans, we make several assumptions. First, we believe that the way in which Asian Americans view the world is influenced by both their family's traditional values (Kim, Atkinson, and Yang, 1999; Sodowsky, Kwan, and Pannu, 1995) and the prevailing attitudes of the environment in which they have been socialized (Sue, Mak, and Sue, 1998). Second, although the current discourse on race has generally been limited to a black-white paradigm (Hune and Chan,

NEW DIRECTIONS FOR STUDENT SERVICES, no. 97, Spring 2002   © Wiley Periodicals, Inc.

1997), Asian Americans have been and remain targets of oppression (Young and Takeuchi, 1998). Our third assumption is that although Asian Americans can and have assumed a variety of leadership roles without learning of the racial legacy of the United States, creating opportunities for gaining an understanding and pride in one's own history may result in a greater sense of a panethnic identity. The development of a panethnic identity has the effect of moving Asian Americans toward involvement in cultural or racial organizations where leadership skills can be developed and expressed but also toward developing a greater sense of personal congruence and fulfillment. Further, for some Asian American students, involvement in these organizations can serve as an entry point to broader campus leadership roles.

Impact of Cultural Values

Cultural values can affect the way that Asian Americans display leadership as well as how Asian Americans are perceived as leaders. Traditional Asian values such as deference to authority, humility, preferring harmony over conflict, and attending to group needs over individual desires contrast with what have traditionally been valued traits of a leader in the United States (Yammarino and Jung, 1998). For example, assertiveness and decisiveness are generally viewed as positive traits for effective leadership, although Asian Americans have been found to be less assertive in comparison to whites (Zane, Sue, Hu, and Kwon, 1991). Asian Americans' leadership style tends to be defined by collaboration and a nonhierarchical nature, which can be viewed as ineffective characteristics of leadership in Western society. In the United States, public speaking and self-confidence are also valued as positive characteristics of student leadership (Astin, 1993), yet Asian cultural values of humility conflict with this individualistic orientation of bringing attention and recognition to oneself. Compounding this conflict is how traditional Asian values, such as deference to a group versus assertiveness and standing on one's own, may be seen as immature by individuals who adhere primarily to Western values. As a result, Asian American students who have internalized these Asian cultural values may view themselves, and also be perceived by others, as less qualified for leadership roles than their white peers or may not even see their contributions as providing leadership.

The retention of Asian values has been observed in even fourth-generation Asian Americans (Min, 1995). Though variation in the adherence to traditional Asian values has been noted (Kim, Atkinson, and Yang, 1999), the little empirical evidence that does exist supports the notion that Asian Americans do maintain some connection to these orientations. While these differences will vary depending on racial identity, gender, acculturation, generational status, access to economic resources, and geographical location (Yeh and Huang, 1996), it is important for practitioners to understand how these values may influence the leadership style of Asian Americans.

Impact of Racism

The authors of this chapter realize that locating differences in leadership style among Asian Americans solely on the basis of adherence to and perceptions of value orientations is simplistic. Further, focusing solely on the adherence to Asian values in leadership situations runs the danger of describing Asian Americans as inherently different and as "other." Thus in addition to gaining an understanding of how Asian cultural values influence leadership styles, it also is important to understand the impact of the campus climate and racism on Asian American involvement in student organizations.

It is not uncommon for Asian Americans to experience taunts and harassment for their physical appearance from their peers (Lee and Zhan, 1998), prejudice and discrimination from college and university administrators (Tan, 1996), and invisibility in K–12 education and postsecondary curricula (Wei, 1993). Asian Americans, like other racial minorities attending traditionally white institutions, have also reported feeling alienated and isolated (Ancis, Sedlacek, and Mohr, 2000; Bennett and Okinaka, 1990; Helm, Sedlacek, and Prieto, 1998; Loo and Rolison, 1986) and dissatisfied with their social relationships (Bennett and Okinaka, 1990). Though Asian Americans continue to experience racism and discrimination, many have not identified it as oppression. Without much exposure to literature or cocurricular opportunities to discuss racism outside the black-white paradigm, many Asian American students are not given the chance to understand fully how their race plays a role in their campus experience. Historically, Asian American students have responded to these situations of discrimination and lack of resources in one of two ways. They have either become active in their community (Omatsu, 1994) and on campus, or they have persisted through their feelings of isolation and alienation (Bennett and Okinaka, 1990).

For some students, the response has been to address these concerns directly with their institution in student leadership roles. In a study to explore reasons for Asian American involvement in student organizations, Liu and Sedlacek (1998) found that "ending racism" and "violence and crime" were cited as the two top issues and concerns to be solved. Realizing the power of one collective voice, Asian American ethnic groups have formed panethnic coalitions (Espiritu, 1992). Many students involved in these panethnic movements have become ardent leaders of their campuses and communities in addressing institutional inequality. For instance, over the past thirty years, Asian American students have demanded responses and provisions for safer campus climates as a result of racial hate crimes and have rallied for Asian American studies programs, resource centers, and increased faculty and staff representation (Omatsu, 1994).

Although some students have responded to discrimination, hate, and lack of resources by becoming more active on campus, others who perceive that their institution's administration as uninterested in their needs may feel misunderstood and as a result be less invested in their campus. In effect, Asian American students may feel disenfranchised to a point where they do not wish to participate in campus life or engage in leadership roles. These students may instead immerse themselves in their academic work and persist in their feelings of alienation until they graduate. Although graduation certainly is a desired outcome, we believe that student affairs practitioners have the responsibility of ensuring that their campus is a positive environment for holistic growth, not just a place to earn a degree.

Practitioners would benefit these students by becoming more open to learning about the issues and feelings of marginality that Asian Americans experience on college campuses today. Further, practitioners could proactively respond to these students' needs by being advocates for the development of Asian American studies curricular and cocurricular programs to develop a sense of community and understanding of their issues. Three particular programs that may engage Asian American students in involvement and leadership roles are described next.

Model Programs

The model programs described here are cocurricular and curricular programs designed to enhance Asian American students' level of understanding of sociopolitical issues and to develop their leadership potential. They are the Asian American Mentoring Program at Pomona College, the Asian American leadership course at the University of Maryland, and Generation APA at the University of Michigan. These programs were selected because they accomplish the following goals:

- They explore how Asian values affect personal leadership styles and how both Asian values and leadership styles relate to a larger sociopolitical context.
- They foster the development of self-concept and confidence as they relate to racial identity.
- They equip students with the knowledge, attitudes, and skills to practice socially responsible leadership in the context of issues of social justice.
- They engage Asian American students in campus life in effective ways.

These programs intentionally create opportunities for Asian Americans to be engaged in activities with their communities, identify themselves as leaders, and ease their transition into campuswide and community leadership roles. In addition, since helping students gain a better understanding of themselves has been found to be important in leadership development (Komives, Lucas, and McMahon, 1998), self-exploration activities are an important part of each of these programs.

Pomona College. The Asian American Mentoring Program at Pomona College trains a group of students to be mentors to first-year students. In the mentors' one-week training program, students attend workshops addressing Asian American history, identity, race and racism, gender roles and sexism, homophobia and heterosexism, and classism. Students also are trained in conflict resolution, communication styles, program planning, facilitation, team building, and other areas that are traditional in leadership training but take Asian American cultural values and issues into account. For example, in the conflict mediation workshop, students consider how Asian cultural values (for example, humility and interdependence) relate to their interpersonal styles. In another workshop, students learn about racial identity development models, explore their own developmental process, and discuss issues and concerns in mentoring first-year students who are at varying statuses of racial identity. Another example of how leadership training is framed in a cultural context is the communication workshop, in which students not only learn to identify the strengths and weaknesses of their personal communication styles but also explore how particular styles such as open, honest, and direct communication are valued in the United States over a nonconfrontational style. Students learn how the valuing of particular styles and behaviors is related to racism, sexism, and larger systems of oppression.

One of the significant outcomes of this program is that students not only learn more about themselves as Asian Americans and leaders but also develop a sociopolitical consciousness. Through their exposure to Asian American history, workshops on identity and oppression, and self-exploration, students gain a sense of empowerment and responsibility to effect social change. They are able to articulate themselves more effectively to one another and to other racial groups about issues of diversity, race and racism, power, privilege, and oppression and explain how these issues relate to their experiences on campus. This increases their confidence level in working with their mentees and communicating with students, faculty, and staff about issues that are viewed as controversial.

University of Maryland. The first Asian American leadership course at the University of Maryland, College Park, was developed in the fall semester 1999 in response to Asian American students' requests that a course on leadership relate to their own specific experience (in contrast to an existing leadership course that better fit the values and culture of white students). In this fifteen-week course, students are provided with an opportunity to think critically about how value orientations, history and current events, and oppression interact to shape the personality and leadership styles of Asian Americans. In addition to in-depth discussions on oppression related to race, social class, gender, and sexual orientation, class periods are devoted to the discussion of power and ethics, organizational development, communication and vision, and interrace relations.

Assignments in the Asian American leadership course include a leadership assessment, active involvement in a student organization, a personal history paper, a "top ten Asian Pacific Americans activists" report, and a report on student perceptions of Asian American leadership and interrace coalition building.

The purpose of the personal history paper is for students to gain a deeper understanding of who they are as leaders in relation to their family and to society. This is often a significant opportunity for students to learn more about themselves and the values and experiences of their parents. Further, students are asked to connect their parents' experiences and values to their own orientations and leadership styles.

For the "top ten APA activists" assignment, students develop and defend a list of their own personal top ten leaders of Asian descent. In completing this project, students gain an understanding and appreciation of the contributions of Asian Pacific Americans in the United States. Because the awareness of contributions of Asian Americans to society is limited, it is often difficult for Asian Americans to identify historical figures, but Asian Americans are not a group without heroes or role models. This project builds a sense of group contribution, group identity and pride, and individual self-efficacy.

Students are also required to be involved actively in a student organization to provide them with an opportunity to apply theory to practice. For instance, students are asked to make observations of group meetings and organizational programming regarding racial and gender dynamics. As a final project, students are required to develop an integrative consultation report including the history of the organization, current organizational structure and dynamics, and recommendations for enhancing the organization.

The classroom activities, paired with the experiential learning, allow for a holistic method in approaching leadership development for Asian American students. The classroom setting permits the instructors to deal directly with issues related to Asian American history, racism, leadership theories, and the impact of culture.

University of Michigan. "Generation APA" was created by the students of the United Asian American Organizations (UAAO) to highlight the many cultural and historical aspects of the Asian Pacific American community. The purpose of Generation APA was to provide a venue where student organizations could come together to mount one collective cultural celebration. By focusing on uniting the APA community, programming spanned ethnic and organizational differences. Featured acts included a step show from an Asian American fraternity, an a cappella performance, and traditional dances from the ethnic organizations. Unique acts, such as culturally fused dances, emerged from this idea of unity. At first glance, these acts may seem like a mere showcasing of Asian culture. However, this program serves as a catalyst for building a sense of panethnic identity among a large number of students who would normally not engage in cocurricular activities beyond their respective ethnic clubs or who might not participate in campus life at all. Generation APA is an example of a developmental program that builds community, collaboration, identity, and leadership in a nonthreatening way. This event also plays a significant role in developing future leaders because it offers an access point for students to gain entrance into the campus community where they can eventually take on formal leadership roles.

Generation APA has grown into a hallmark program for the development of a collective APA identity at the University of Michigan. Since Generation APA is completely student-run, students gain experience with production, management, teamwork, group building, and conflict resolution. Through participating in this event, students gain a sense of panethnic identity and purpose. For students who may be members of specific ethnic organizations, working on this program allows for interaction across ethnic lines. Through the planning of this event, South Asian Americans may come to realize that they share similarities with Pilipino Americans not just in terms of cultural values but also in their being racialized under one umbrella.

In organizing this show, planners also must ask themselves questions about what Asian Pacific American means, who is included in this definition, and how to develop an event that is both political and cultural. Generation APA has become a tool by which students have the opportunity to dialogue, explore, and challenge one another on notions of race and ethnicity and how they are defined in the United States. As students struggle with and explore these challenging issues, they gain insight and security with their identity as APAs.

Conclusion

In fostering the leadership potential of Asian American students, student affairs professionals need to be cognizant of the ways in which cultural values influence how leadership is perceived and displayed differently among various groups of people. Student affairs practitioners should not treat leadership as "culture-free" or independent of larger issues of race and racism in the United States but rather must infuse these concepts into developing opportunities for students to explore their identity and leadership styles in a cultural context. Further, student affairs practitioners should work proactively to engage Asian American students in the life of their respective campuses, whether in traditional leadership roles, activism, or innovative leadership programs as described in this chapter. Being sensitive to cultural differences and challenging the biases inherent in our understanding of leadership can help support and encourage both greater campus involvement and development of leadership among Asian American students.

References

Ancis, J. R., Sedlacek, W. E., and Mohr, J. J. "Student Perceptions of Campus Cultural Climate by Race." *Journal of Counseling and Development*, 2000, 78, 180–185.

Astin, A. W. "An Empirical Typology of College Students." *Journal of College Student Development*, 1993, 34, 36–46.

Bennett, C. E., and Okinaka, A. M. "Factors Related to Persistence Among Asian, Black, Hispanic, and White Undergraduates at a Predominantly White University:

Comparison Between First- and Fourth-Year Cohorts." *Urban Review*, 1990, *22*, 33–60.

Espiritu, Y. L. *Asian American Panethnicity: Bridging Institutions and Identities.* Philadelphia: Temple University Press, 1992.

Goto, S. "Asian Americans and Developmental Relationships." In A. J. Murrell and F. J. Crosby (eds.), *Mentoring Dilemmas: Developmental Relationships Within Multicultural Organizations—Applied Social Research*. Mahwah, N.J.: Erlbaum, 1999.

Helm, E. G., Sedlacek, W. E., and Prieto, D. O. "The Relationship Between Attitudes Toward Diversity and Overall Satisfaction of University Students by Race." *Journal of College Counseling*, 1998, *1*, 111–120.

Hune, S., and Chan, K. S. "Special Focus: Asian Pacific American Demographic and Educational Trends." In D. J. Carter and R. Wilson (eds.), *Fifteenth Annual Status Report on Minorities in Higher Education, 1996–1997*. Washington, D.C.: American Council on Education, 1997.

Kim, B.S.K., Atkinson, D. R., and Yang, P. H. "The Asian Values Scale: Development, Factor Analysis, Validation, and Reliability." *Journal of Counseling Psychology*, 1999, *46*, 342–352.

Komives, S. R., Lucas, N., and McMahon, T. R. *Exploring Leadership: For College Students Who Want to Make a Difference.* San Francisco: Jossey-Bass, 1998.

Lee, L. C., and Zhan, G. "Psychosocial Status of Children and Youths." In L. C. Lee and N.W.S. Zane (eds.), *Handbook of Asian American Psychology.* Thousand Oaks, Calif.: Sage, 1998.

Liu, W. M., and Sedlacek, W. E. "Differences in Leadership and Co-Curricular Perception Among Entering Male and Female Asian Pacific American College Students." *Journal of the Freshman-Year Experience*, 1998, *11*, 93–114.

Loo, C., and Rolison, G. "Alienation of Ethnic Minority Students at a Predominantly White University." *Journal of Higher Education*, 1986, *57*, 58–77.

Min, P. G. *Asian Americans: Contemporary Issues and Trends.* Thousand Oaks, Calif.: Sage, 1995.

Omatsu, G. "The 'Four Prisons' and the Movements of Liberation: Asian American Activism from the 1960s to the 1990s." In K. Aguilar–San Juan (ed.), *The State of Asian America: Activism and Resistance in the 1990s.* Boston: South End Press, 1994.

Sodowsky, G. R., Kwan, K.-L. K., and Pannu, R. "Ethnic Identity of Asians in the United States." In J. G. Ponterotto, J. M. Casas, L. A. Suzuki, and C. M. Alexander (eds.), *Handbook of Multicultural Counseling.* Thousand Oaks, Calif.: Sage, 1995.

Sue, D., Mak, W. S., and Sue, D. W. "Ethnic Identity." In L. C. Lee and N.W.S. Zane (eds.), *Handbook of Asian American Psychology.* Thousand Oaks, Calif.: Sage, 1998.

Tan, D. L. "Uniqueness of the Asian American Experience in Higher Education." *College Student Journal*, 1996, *28*, 412–421.

Wei, W. *The Asian American Movement.* Philadelphia: Temple University Press, 1993.

Yammarino, F. J., and Jung, D. I. "Asian Americans and Leadership." *Journal of Applied Behavioral Science*, 1998, *34*, 47–68.

Yeh, C. J., and Huang, K. "The Collectivistic Nature of Ethnic Identity Development Among Asian American College Students." *Adolescence*, 1996, *31*, 645–661.

Young, K., and Takeuchi, D. T. "Racism." In L. C. Lee and N.W.S. Zane (eds.), *Handbook of Asian American Psychology.* Thousand Oaks, Calif.: Sage, 1998.

Zane, N.W.S., Sue, S., Hu, L., and Kwon, J. H. "Asian American Assertion: A Social Learning Analysis of Cultural Differences." *Journal of Counseling Psychology*, 1991, *38*, 63–70.

CHRISTOPHER T. H. LIANG *is a doctoral student in counseling psychology and instructor in Asian American studies, University of Maryland, College Park.*

SUNNY LEE *is assistant director, Cross-Cultural Center, University of California, Irvine.*

MARIE P. TING *is a doctoral student in the higher education program, University of Maryland, College Park.*

9

The authors identify challenges for student affairs professionals and suggest responses and questions for more effective work with Asian American students.

Epilogue

Charlene Chew-Ogi, Alan Yoshiharu Ogi

A decade and a half ago, we penned words that expressed our fervent desire to see established a strong body of literature, opinion, and personal experience on the subject of Asian American students on college campuses (Chew and Ogi, 1987). We attempted to voice an Asian American consciousness and declare the need for additional research and opinions on Asian American students. As products of the collegiate machine of the 1970s and 1980s, we realized, at first hand, the need for unique, specialized services to be afforded to the new immigrant communities of Asian Pacific Americans, as well as to the well-established Asian American groups on college campuses. This issue of *New Directions for Student Services* responds by addressing a broad spectrum of issues facing Asian American college students, but we hope that this is only the beginning of the groundwork for additional research, theory, practical applications, and discussions about Asian Americans in higher education. We hope that manuscripts continue to be written from both theoretical and practical perspectives to satisfy a wide audience in the academic and student affairs professions. We take this opportunity to express the challenge to all providers of knowledge and services to heed these words attributed to Albert Einstein: "Problems cannot be solved with the same level of consciousness that created them."

Since we wrote our original article in 1987, some changes have occurred in some of our institutions with regard to the success of Asian Americans. In the past fifteen years, we have experienced an increase in Asian American enrollment in college. We have seen a few Asian Americans rise to positions in the upper levels of administration, but they face tremendous challenges, and their numbers are not close to the proportion of Asian American students on campus. We have seen the rise of Asian American studies programs across the country, as well as specialized Asian American student services and cultural centers.

However, even now at the beginning of the twenty-first century, we observe a resurgence of the "yellow peril" in our media and in the heart of our educational system. We have seen Asian Americans caught in the middle of battles over racial politics, affirmative action, and college admissions. Asian Americans continue to experience discrimination as well as verbal and physical assaults. Anti-Asian hate crimes are on the rise. There is more attention to what kung fu movie is at the box office than on what Asian American students are contributing to their campuses and their communities. So how far have we really come?

The Challenges

Colleges and universities find themselves in a landscape of more knowledge than humankind has ever known. Belief systems are being challenged. Student affairs and academia are not working with students from a singular culture. The United States is changing demographically as many more ethnic groups are found in this country. With the focus on Asian American college students in this volume, what do we learn? We find that Asian Americans have achieved "critical mass" in some areas of the general population and are prominent on certain campuses throughout our nation. How sensitive and prepared are we for the needs of Asian American students as they matriculate through our system?

As we learn from Shirley Hune in Chapter Two, census data homogenize Asian American students and conceal the distinctions of individuals and groups that need attention. We must be vigilant in analyzing statistics and understand that Asian Americans as a whole are "bimodal" in that both sides of the educational scale are represented in this population, a point emphasized by Theresa Ling Yeh in her discussion of at-risk Asian American students in Chapter Six. We must realize that for every Asian American student who seems to have the academic, social, and financial support and the ability to navigate our system of higher education, there is another who needs a great deal of support to succeed. We must go beyond the model minority myth and take a closer look at the backgrounds and experiences of the Asian American students on our campuses.

We learn from Bob Suzuki in Chapter Three that the model minority stereotype continues to be applied to Asian American students in subtle ways, resulting in high expectations for Asian American students and assumptions that they are doing well when in fact they may be struggling. Thus the educational needs and concerns of many Asian American students are ignored. Suzuki also discusses the negative image of the "perfidious foreigner," which may result in alienation. Without our efforts at understanding and challenging these images, these stereotypes can have a lasting and detrimental impact on the collegiate experiences of Asian Americans.

As student affairs professionals, we must check our personal commitment to diversity and our understanding of Asian American students. We need to be continually critical and reflective with respect to our work. What do we know about the Asian American students on our campuses? What kinds of services are we providing for them? How well are their needs being met, and what is our evidence? Are we doing all that we can to improve the racial climate of our offices and campuses? Do our staffs reflect the student diversity of our institutions? When conducting a search, who on the committee is Asian American or understands Asian American perspectives? Do we have positive role models for Asian American students on our campuses? If we respect the value of diversity, we need to ensure that it is reflected in our philosophy, staff, programs, and day-to-day operations. Too often a program is cut, sending a message to Asian American students that they are not important, as eloquently pointed out by Angela, Bao, and Sophia, the three student writers of Chapter One. Thus we need to listen to Asian American students and understand them from their perspective.

How do we do that? How can we learn to listen in meaningful ways? How can we put aside our own cultural perspectives and experiences to understand Asian American students who may experience the institution as a poor fit? How do we seek out Asian American students and show them that we want to know and understand their needs and experiences?

Responses

How do we respond and improve our practice for Asian American students? First, we must understand our own values and realize that our students may not share them because they come from different cultural backgrounds. The challenge for many Asian American students is that they come to institutions that value individual achievement and survival of the fittest. However, the voices from their hearts tell them that they are pursuing higher education to bring honor to their family by what they learn from elders at the college or university. Asian American students are looking for guidance, but few members of the institution understand the cultural conflicts that these students encounter on campus.

As student affairs professionals, we have an understanding of the institution's culture and traditions and thus may be able to help students understand the conflicts they are experiencing. For students to have an ally to help them look at options and choices is an important element in providing support for them and enhancing their college experiences. However, for professionals who say that they don't know their own culture, it may be a challenge to be an ally to those who have a stronger sense of culture. To be an effective ally, we need not only understand the student's perspective but also understand our own prejudices and biases. How do the stereotypes of Asian Americans affect the ways in which we view these students, the services we think they need, and the ways in which we measure their development and satisfaction on campus? We must also guard against seeing Asian Americans only through a "race lens" and remember that they may also be multiracial, gay, lesbian, bisexual, transgender, or differently abled. Our ability to hear out their needs over our own preconceived beliefs is an important skill.

Knowing, for example, that Asian Americans are often subject to great influence by parents and family, student affairs professionals need to consider the role of family dynamics in a way that differs from how we have been trained (which is often to presume that students should separate psychologically from their parents and should make decisions for themselves). We need to understand that Asian American students see themselves as individuals but also as an integral part of a family, a duality that does not always fit neatly into a Western frame of reference.

An underlying conflict between many Asian American students and today's institutions of higher education is a difference in emphasis: these students are focused on family, group, and community, whereas our colleges and universities tend to be focused on the individual and competition. As noted by many of the chapter authors, this conflict can have a great impact on students' sense of self, identity, involvement on campus, and understanding of identity—not to mention how they may be perceived by others. Asian American students who sense that they are not understood by the institution can feel discouraged, marginalized, and alone. Success for Asian American students on a college campus can feel like adapting to all the values of the institution. Students, however, should not feel that they must give up who they are in order to be successful or involved in college. Thus developing a deeper understanding of themselves in relation to family, culture, and society can provide students with a more comprehensive and holistic understanding of external influences that may be affecting their experiences.

In addition to examining external influences such as family and culture, several authors challenge us to recognize the developmental and psychosocial implications of race and racism. Alvin Alvarez urges us to understand racial identity for Asian Americans in Chapter Four and reminds us that college may be a dissonance-inducing environment that underscores the salience of race. The authors of Chapter Five emphasize the influence of racism and of racial identity on psychosocial development. Race and racism can lead to student involvement and activism or, conversely, apathy, as pointed out by the students in Chapter One and by the authors of Chapter Eight.

This holistic perspective extends to the classroom as well, as Alvarez and William Liu in Chapter Seven point out the need for academic and nonacademic programs and services to support each other. As more academic areas are engaged in interdisciplinary collaboration within and outside their institutions, these partnerships can be continued in new and interesting ways, such as between Asian American studies and student affairs. Continuing to base services on dualistic conceptualizations of student needs (intellectual versus psychosocial) and student experiences (in-class versus out-of-class) disregards the complexity of students' development.

As the number of Asian American students increases at colleges and universities, a stronger voice is growing that the university is not meeting their needs. The students featured in Chapter One are typical of students who are beginning to speak out. This activism is important, as Asian Americans are often given a subtle message that being reserved, quiet, and unassuming are good traits to have and embrace, and so the cultural belief of "not bringing shame to the family" keeps many Asian Pacific Americans from voicing dissent. Thus many student affairs professionals are not aware of the dissatisfaction or difficulties that these students are experiencing. Many chapters in this volume speak to the need to understand how we can empower and foster growth in these Asian American students, who tend not to feel comfortable asking for or demanding rights in the same ways as other students. Many Asian American cultures value respect for authority or being humble; this can mean that actively speaking out may feel uncomfortable or require a lot of support. Empowerment may mean helping students navigate the collegiate environment, learn more about racism, explore their cultural backgrounds, expand definitions of leadership, and move beyond the confines of individual institutions to collaborate with regional and even national organizations. The more we know and understand Asian American students, the better allies and advocates we can be to this overlooked and often misunderstood population.

The Next Step

The chapters in this volume remind us to look beyond the simplicity of aggregated data, which is particularly important as we attempt a shift in thinking that is more inclusive, more aware, and more challenging. We recognize issues inclusive of lifestyle differences, religious beliefs, abilities and disabilities, and socioeconomic differences among our Asian American community; the identity challenges of being of mixed heritages; the opening of arms to those adopted into families of different cultures; the decline of some Asian American communities; and the acculturation, assimilation, and intergenerational challenges facing today's Asian American students.

Understanding and providing services for Asian American students is challenging, in light of the constantly changing nature of this population. In working with Asian American students, we have found a varied need for services, role models, opportunities in leadership, understanding of personal heritage, and struggles with identity. Yet this complexity should not keep us from moving forward and trying to improve our programs and services.

We must all work through our thoughts and feelings to come up with creative alternatives. As Einstein purportedly said, "We must think outside the structures that create the challenges." This is not an easy task when thinking of the sacred cows and traditions of our collegiate systems (such as the focus on residential students, the wealth of services for Greek systems, and alumni traditions) that may not have meaning or relevance to Asian American students. However, we are at a turning point where no longer should the dominant campus culture cater to or be identified with any particular group of people.

As you reflect on this volume, think about how the various chapters relate to the Asian American students on your campus, and adapt the information here to fit the needs of your department and institution. Learn the demographics of Asian Americans on your campus; get to know these students, their experiences, their hopes and dreams. Attend an Asian American student organization meeting or event, and learn what issues are important to those leaders on your campus. Get to know the Asian American students who may work in your office or sit in your classrooms. Share the information you have learned here with your colleagues, attend conference presentations, and read other research that can help you explore and understand the issues relevant to your work.

Remember Suzuki's suggestions for developing a comprehensive plan for our campuses in terms of Asian American students. We need to engage in dialogue with our Asian American students and seek to understand their background, their culture, and what they want from their college experience. We need to listen, empower, and challenge. We need to create safe spaces on campus that students like Angela, Bao, and Sophia so value as they deal with the many issues they face as Asian American students. Remember their thoughts, hopes, and suggestions as you continue to learn about, understand, and advocate for today's Asian American college students.

Reference

Chew, C. A., and Ogi, A. Y. "Asian American College Student Perspectives." In D. J. Wright (ed.), *Responding to the Needs of Today's Minority Students.* New Directions for Student Services, no. 38. San Francisco: Jossey-Bass, 1987.

CHARLENE CHEW-OGI *is director, Office of Residential Life, Housing and Residential Services, University of California, Santa Barbara.*

ALAN YOSHIHARU OGI *is assistant director, Housing and Residential Services, University of California, Santa Barbara.*

10

The authors identify Asian American associations and organizations, academic journals, periodicals, and media resources. Selected annotated resources on Asian American activism and politics, counseling and psychology, educational issues, gender and sexual orientation, history, policy reports, and racial and ethnic identity are also included.

Additional Resources on Asian Americans

Corinne Maekawa Kodama, Sunny Lee, Christopher T. H. Liang, Alvin N. Alvarez, Marylu K. McEwen

General Resources

Associations and Organizations. Although there are many regional and ethnic-specific organizations, we have listed those that are most pan-Asian and national in scope, have a long history or large membership base, or have strong educational programs and resources.

Asian American Legal Defense and Education Fund (AALDEF), 99 Hudson Street, 12th floor, New York, NY 10013; (212) 966–5932; aaldef@worldnet.att.net

Asian Pacific Americans in Higher Education (APAHE), c/o Gene Awakuni, Stanford University, 459 Lagunita Drive, Suite 6, Stanford, CA 94305; (650) 725–1808; awakuni@standford.edu

Asian Pacific American Institute for Congressional Studies, 209 Pennsylvania Avenue S.E., Suite 100, Washington, DC 20003; (202) 547–9100; www.apaics.org

Association of Asian American Studies, c/o Gary Okihiro, Cornell University, Ithaca, NY 14853

Committee Against Anti-Asian Violence, 191 East Third Street, New York, NY 10009; (212) 473–6485; caaav@dti.net

Japanese American Citizens League, 1765 Sutter Street, San Francisco, CA 94115; (415) 921–5225; www.jacl.org

Leadership Education for Asian Pacifics (LEAP), 327 East Second Street, Suite 226, Los Angeles, CA 90012; (213) 485–1422; www.leap.org

NEW DIRECTIONS FOR STUDENT SERVICES, no. 97, Spring 2002 © Wiley Periodicals, Inc.

National Asian Pacific American Legal Consortium, 1140 Connecticut Avenue N.W., Suite 1200, Washington, DC 20036; (202) 296–2300; www.napalc.org

National Coalition for Asian Pacific American Community Development, 1001 Connecticut Avenue N.W., Suite 704, Washington, DC 20036; (202) 223–2442; www.nationalcapacd.org

Organization of Chinese Americans, 1001 Connecticut Avenue N.W., Suite 601, Washington, DC 20036; (202) 223–5500; www.ocanatl.org

White House Initiative on Asian Americans and Pacific Islanders, 5600 Fishers Lane, Room 10–42, Rockville, MD 20857; (301) 443–2492; www.aapi.gov; aapi@hrsa.gov

Academic Journals. *Amerasia Journal*

Oldest academic journal in Asian American studies. Focuses on interdisciplinary research of scholarship, criticism, and literature. Published at UCLA Asian American Studies Center three times a year. Contact: (310) 825–2968; www.sscnet.ucla/edu/esp/aasc; ku@ucla.edu

Journal of Asian American Policy Review

Focuses on public policy issues affecting Asian Americans. Edited by graduate students at Harvard and Berkeley and published by the John F. Kennedy School of Government at Harvard University. Contact: (617) 496–8655; aapr@harvard.edu

Journal of Asian American Studies

Official publication of the Association for Asian American Studies. Explores all aspects of the Asian American experience and publishes original works of scholarly interest. Contact: Johns Hopkins University Press, (800) 548–1784.

Other Periodicals. *A Magazine*

Bimonthly, pan-Asian magazine with the largest circulation in the United States. Seeks to be the media voice and forum for Asian American issues and views. Broad coverage of political and social issues, notable APAs, and popular culture. Contact: (212) 593–8089 (ext. 21); www.aonline.com; amag@amagazine.com

AsianWeek

English-language newsweekly for the pan-Asian community. Dedicated to chronicling the Asian American experience, providing a national forum on issues important to Asian Americans, and creating a stronger political voice for Asian Americans. Contact: (415) 397–0220; www.asianweek.com/AsianWeek

Media Resources. Asian American Curriculum Project

For over thirty years has provided one of most comprehensive collections of Asian American and ethnic-specific books and education materials. Contact: 83 Thirty-Seventh Avenue, San Mateo, CA 94403; (800) 874–2242; www.asianamericanbooks.com

National Asian American Telecommunications Association

Key distributor and exhibitor of Asian and Asian American films and videos. Extensive catalogue of more than two hundred titles. Special discounts to educators. Contact: 346 Ninth Street, 2nd floor, San Francisco, CA 94103; (415) 863–0814; www.naatanet.org

Some journal and media sources may be difficult to find unless one is in a metropolitan area with a large concentration of Asian Americans.

Resources by Topic

Activism and Politics. Aguilar–San Juan, K. (ed.). *The State of Asian America: Activism and Resistance in the 1990s.* Boston: South End Press, 1994.

Essays on the history of Asian American activism from the 1960s to the 1990s, including feminism, the arts, anti-Asian bias, domestic violence, labor, and Asian American studies.

Espiritu, Y. L. *Asian American Panethnicity: Bridging Institutions and Identities.* Philadelphia: Temple University Press, 1994.

Discusses central issues, challenges, and successes of the development of pan-Asian political identity out of diverse Asian American ethnic groups.

Fong, T. P. *The Contemporary Asian American Experience: Beyond the Model Minority.* Upper Saddle River, N.J.: Prentice Hall, 1998.

Broad analysis of Asian American experience from a journalistic sociological approach. Topics include contemporary history, culture, theoretical perspectives, and data on immigration, demographics, and education.

Wei, W. *The Asian American Movement.* Philadelphia: Temple University Press, 1993.

Comprehensive discussion of Asian American activism from the late 1960s to the early 1990s in the areas of identity politics, the women's movement, the alternative press, Asian American studies, community-based efforts, and electoral politics.

Zia, H. *Asian American Dreams: The Emergence of an American People.* New York: Farrar, Straus & Giroux, 2000.

A sociohistorical biography of the transformation of Asian Americans; examines student movements, racism, generational issues, affirmative action, popular culture, and human rights.

Counseling and Psychology. Lee, E. (ed.). *Working with Asian Americans: A Guide for Clinicians.* New York: Guilford, 1997.
Topics related to counseling Asian Americans, including chapters on specific ethnicities, age groups, and mental health issues.

Lee, L. C., and Zane, N.W.S. (eds.). *Handbook of Asian American Psychology.* Thousand Oaks, Calif.: Sage, 1998.
Comprehensive overview of Asian American psychology, with analyses of topics such as Asian American elderly, children and youth, family violence, interracial marriages, ethnic identity, and addictive behaviors.

Leong, F.T.L., and Whitfield, J. R. *Asians in the United States: Abstracts of the Psychological and Behavioral Literature, 1967–1991.* Washington, D.C.: American Psychological Association, 1992.
Annotated bibliography of journal articles, dissertations, books, and book chapters based on searches of PsycINFO, PsycLit, and *Dissertation Abstracts.*

Sandhu, D. (ed.). *Asian and Pacific Islander Americans: Issues and Concerns in Counseling and Psychotherapy.* Huntington, N.Y.: Nova Science Publishers, 1999.
Topics include transracial adoption, substance abuse, women's issues, racial identity, and ethnic identity.

Uba, L. *Asian Americans: Personality Patterns, Identity, and Mental Health.* New York: Guilford, 1994.
Chapters on stress, refugee status, psychopathology, psychotherapy, and underuse of mental health services among Asian Americans.

Educational Issues. "Asian and Pacific Americans: Behind the Myths." *Change,* Nov.-Dec. 1989.
Special issue on Asian Americans in higher education, including research articles, commentary, and case studies. Topics include the model minority, demographics of Asian Americans in higher education, and admissions.

Chew, C. A., and Ogi, A. Y. "Asian American College Student Perspectives." In D. J. Wright (ed.), *Responding to the Needs of Today's Minority Students.* New Directions for Student Services, no. 38. San Francisco: Jossey-Bass, 1987.
One of first articles focusing on Asian Americans as a unique student population in higher education, still cited frequently.

Hirabayashi, L. R. (ed.). *Teaching Asian America: Diversity and the Problem of Community*. Lanham, Md.: Rowman & Littlefield, 1998.

Essays about pedagogical, ethical, philosophical, and social psychological issues that concern Asian American studies; helpful for practitioners interested in developing curricular or cocurricular programs for Asian American students.

Kiang, R. N. "Issues of Curriculum and Community for First-Generation Asian Americans in College." In L. S. Zwerling and H. B. London (eds.), *First-Generation Students: Confronting the Cultural Issues*. New Directions for Community Colleges, no. 80. San Francisco: Jossey-Bass, 1992.

Based on interviews, describes first-generation students' experiences with college majors, influence of gender, and barriers of language, social isolation, family responsibilities, and racism.

Nakanishi, D. T., and Nishida, T. Y. (eds.). *The Asian American Educational Experience: A Source Book for Teachers and Students*. New York: Routledge, 1995.

Collection of articles (some previously published) on Asian Americans in education. Major topics include schooling of Asian Americans, academic achievement and model minority debate, K–12 issues, and higher education.

Takagi, D. Y. *The Retreat from Race: Asian-American Admissions and Racial Politics*. New Brunswick, N.J.: Rutgers University Press, 1992.

Highlights political battles over Asian Americans and college admission policies, particularly in the 1980s. In-depth discussion of affirmative action and Asian Americans, the model minority myth, and the politics of representation.

Yee, J. A., and Kuo, E. W. "Bibliographic Review Essay: The Experiences of Asian Pacific Americans in Higher Education." *Journal of Asian American Studies*, 2000, 3(1), 101–110.

Summarizes articles from the 1990s addressing policies and practices, students' experiences, admissions and affirmative action, faculty and tenure, women in higher education, and pedagogy and curriculum.

Gender and Sexual Orientation. Asian Women United of California. *Making Waves: An Anthology of Writings by and About Asian American Women*. Boston: Beacon Press, 1989.

Kim, E. H., Villanueva, L. V., and Asian Women United of California. *Making More Waves: New Writing by Asian American Women*. Boston: Beacon Press, 1997.

Poems, stories, and essays by women on topics such as immigration, war, work, injustice, reflection, and activism.

Chow, C. S. *Leaving Deep Water: The Lives of Asian American Women at the Crossroads of Two Cultures.* New York: Dutton, 1998.

Draws on personal experiences of Asian American women related to the academic, career, and social expectations of parents, cultural identity, and relationships with parents.

Espiritu, Y. L. *Asian American Women and Men: Labor, Laws, and Love.* Thousand Oaks, Calif.: Sage, 1997.

Gendered analyses of historical and contemporary issues of relationships between Asian American women and men in the context of race, social class, ethnicity, labor conditions, and immigration.

Hune, S. *Asian Pacific American Women in Higher Education: Claiming Visibility and Voice.* Washington, D.C.: Association of American Colleges and Universities, 1998.

Report on educational participation, experiences, and biases faced by Asian Pacific American women students, staff, administrators, and faculty; recommendations for policy and practice in higher education.

Leong, R. (ed.). *Asian American Sexualities: Dimensions of the Gay and Lesbian Experience.* New York: Routledge, 1996.

Addresses the intersection of sexual orientation and race for Asian Americans; provides perspectives of Asian American gay, lesbian, and bisexual authors on their personal and political identities.

Shah, S. (ed.). *Dragon Ladies: Asian American Feminists Breathe Fire.* Boston: South End Press, 1997.

Essays on issues such as resistance, health, work, domestic violence, and spirituality.

History. Chan, S. *Asian Americans: An Interpretive History.* Boston: Twayne, 1991.

Detailed and comprehensive history of Asian Americans from the mid-nineteenth century to the 1990s.

Takaki, R. *Strangers from a Different Shore: A History of Asian Americans.* (rev. ed.) New York: Little, Brown, 1998.

Revision of a landmark work; interweaves personal narratives with historical facts and events; chapters highlight specific Asian ethnic groups in the United States.

Policy Reports. Hune, S., and Chan, K. S. "Special Focus: Asian Pacific American Demographic and Educational Trends." In D. J. Carter and R. Wilson (eds.), *Fifteenth Annual Status Report on Minorities in Higher Education.* Washington, D.C.: American Council on Education, 1997.

Leadership Education for Asian Pacifics (LEAP), Asian Pacific American Public Policy Institute, and UCLA Asian American Studies Center. *The State of Asian Pacific America: Policy Issues to the Year 2020. A Public Policy Report.* Los Angeles: LEAP, 1993.

Leadership Education for Asian Pacifics (LEAP) and Asian Pacific American Public Policy Institute. *The State of Asian Pacific America: Transforming Race Relations.* Los Angeles: LEAP, 2000.

National Asian Pacific American Legal Consortium. *1999 Audit of Anti-Asian Violence: Challenging the Invisibility of Hate.* Washington, D. C.: National Asian Pacific American Legal Consortium, 1999.

U.S. Bureau of the Census. *We the American: Asians.* Washington, D.C.: U.S. Government Printing Office, 1993.

U.S. Bureau of the Census. *We the American: Pacific Islanders.* Washington, D.C.: U.S. Government Printing Office, 1993.

U.S. Commission on Civil Rights. *Civil Rights Issues Facing Asian Americans in the 1990s: A Report of the United States Commission on Civil Rights.* Washington D.C.: U.S. Commission on Civil Rights, 1992.

Racial and Ethnic Identity. Lee, L. C. (ed.). *Asian Americans: Collages of Identities.* Ithaca, N.Y.: Asian American Studies Program, Cornell University, 1992.
    Perspectives of sixteen Asian American writers on ethnic and racial identities.

Lee, S. J. *Unraveling the "Model Minority" Stereotype: Listening to Asian American Youth.* New York: Teachers College Press, 1996.
    Results of a year spent with Asian American high school students in New York. Focuses on identity and peer relationships, framed in the context of four distinctive Asian and Asian American cliques.

Root, M.P.P. (ed.). *Racially Mixed People in America.* Thousand Oaks, Calif.: Sage, 1992.
    Chapters on Vietnamese Amerasians, interracial Japanese Americans, and binational Amerasians.

Root, M.P.P. (ed.). *The Multiracial Experience: Racial Borders as the New Frontier.* Thousand Oaks, Calif.: Sage, 1996.
    Chapters on multiracial Japanese Americans, biracial Korean-white experience, and multiracial Asian American lesbians.

Sodowsky, G. R., Kwan, K.-L. K., and Pannu, R. "Ethnic Identity of Asians in the United States." In J. G. Ponterotto, J. M. Casas, L. A. Suzuki, and C. M. Alexander (eds.), *Handbook of Multicultural Counseling.* Thousand Oaks, Calif.: Sage, 1995.
  Considers multidimensional components of ethnic identity for Asian Americans; identifies internal and external aspects of ethnic identity.

Tuan, M. *Forever Foreigners or Honorary Whites? The Asian Ethnic Experience Today.* New Brunswick, N.J.: Rutgers University Press, 1998.
  Qualitative study of middle-class, third-generation or later Chinese Americans and Japanese Americans regarding ethnic identity, experiences with racism and discrimination, and perspectives toward contemporary issues of Asian Americans.

CORINNE MAEKAWA KODAMA *is assistant director, Office of Career Services, University of Illinois, Chicago.*

SUNNY LEE *is assistant director, Cross-Cultural Center, University of California, Irvine.*

CHRISTOPHER T. H. LIANG *is a doctoral student in counseling psychology and instructor in Asian American studies, University of Maryland, College Park.*

ALVIN N. ALVAREZ *is assistant professor and coordinator of the college counseling program, Department of Counseling, San Francisco State University, San Francisco, California.*

MARYLU K. MCEWEN *is associate professor in college student personnel, Department of Counseling and Personnel Services, University of Maryland, College Park.*

ERRATA

On the title page of *New Directions for Student Services,* no. 96 (Winter 2001), the affiliation of editors Larry H. Dietz and Ernest J. Enchelmayer should have been listed as Southern Illinois University Carbondale.

In *NDSS,* no. 95, in Chapter One ("Spirituality and Student Development: Theoretical Connections," by Patrick G. Love), a list from Chapter Two was erroneously inserted. The first two paragraphs under the subhead "Faith Development and Student Development," pp. 8–9, should have appeared as follows:

Parks (2000) presents a three-component model of faith development. The three interacting components she describes are forms of knowing (cognitive aspects of faith development), forms of dependence (an affective aspect of faith development), and forms of community (social aspects of faith development). The cognitive component is grounded in the work of William Perry (1970) and James Fowler (1981), and the forms of knowing and their development correspond with the structures posited by Perry, Fowler, and other cognitive-structural theorists. Fowler's theory describes seven stages of faith development that cover the life span. The four stages most likely to be experienced by college students are mythic-literal, synthetic-conventional, individuative-reflective, and conjunctive.

Parks describes forms of dependence as affective aspects of faith development; they focus on how people feel. However, in her description of the various stages of dependence she also describes interpersonal interactions, which are social aspects of development, and the view of oneself as an authority figure, which is an aspect of cognitive development. She describes the dependence part of her model as focusing on the relationships through which we discover and change our views of knowledge and faith. More than the other two elements of her model, the forms of dependence demonstrate the interactive nature of the components of her model.

INDEX

Back Issue/Subscription Order Form

Copy or detach and send to:
Jossey-Bass, A Wiley Company, 989 Market Street, San Francisco CA 94103-1741

Call or fax tollfree: Phone 888-378-2537 6AM-5PM PST; Fax 800-605-2665

Back issues: Please send me the following issues at $27 each
(Important: please include series initials and issue number, such as SS94)

1. SS _____

_____

_____

$ _____Total for single issues

$ _____ SHIPPING CHARGES: SURFACE

	Domestic	Canadian
First Item	$5.00	$6.50
Each Add'l Item	$3.00	$3.00

For next-day and second-day delivery rates, call the number listed above.

Subscriptions   Please ❏ start ❏ renew my subscription to *New Directions for Student Services* for the year 2_____ at the following rate:

U.S.	❏ Individual $65	❏ Institutional $130
Canada	❏ Individual $65	❏ Institutional $170
All Others	❏ Individual $89	❏ Institutional $204

$ _____Total single issues and subscriptions (Add appropriate sales tax for your state for single issue orders. No sales tax for U.S. subscriptions. Canadian residents, add GST for subscriptions and single issues.)

Federal Tax ID 135593032   GST 89102 8052

❏ Payment enclosed (U.S. check or money order only)

❏ VISA, MC, AmEx, Discover Card # _____ Exp. date_____

Signature _____ Day phone _____

❏ Bill me (U.S. institutional orders only. Purchase order required)

Purchase order #_____

Name _____

Address _____

_____

Phone_____ E-mail _____

For more information about Jossey-Bass, visit our Web site at: www.josseybass.com

PROMOTION CODE = ND3

Save Now on the Best of ABOUT CAMPUS Series Sets Enriching the Student Learning Experience

Dedicated to the idea that student learning is the responsibility of all educators on campus, **About Campus** illuminates critical issues faced by both student affairs and academic affairs staff as they work on the shared goal that brought them to the same campus in the first place: to help students learn.

With each issue, **About Campus** combines the imagination and creativity found in the best magazines and the authority and thoughtfulness found in the best professional journals. Now we've taken the four most popular issues from three volume years and we've made them available as a set— at a tremendous savings over our $20.00 single issue price.

Best of About Campus – Volume 3

Facts and Myths About Assessment in Student Affairs – Why Learning Communities? Why Now? – The Stressed Student: How Can We Help? – Being All That We Can Be
ISBN 0–7879–6128–0 $12.00

Best of About Campus – Volume 4

Increasing Expectations for Student Effort – The Matthew Shepard Tragedy: Crisis and Beyond – Civic and Moral Learning – Faculty-Student Affairs Collaboration on Assessment.
ISBN 0–7879–6129–9 $12.00

Best of About Campus – Volume 5

The Diversity Within – What Can We Do About Student Cheating – Bonfire: Tragedy and Tradition – Hogwarts: The Learning Community.
ISBN 0–7879–6130–2 $12.00

To order by phone: call 1–800–956–7739 or 415–433–1740
Visit our website at www.josseybass.com

Use promotion code **ND2** to guarantee your savings.
Shipping and applicable taxes will be added.

ABOUT CAMPUS

Sponsored by the *American College Personnel Association*
Published by Jossey-Bass, A Wiley Company

Patricia M. King, Executive Editor
Jon C. Dalton, Senior Editor

Published bimonthly. Individual subscriptions $53.00. Institutional subscriptions $95.00.

Jossey-Bass, A Wiley Company • 989 Market St., Fifth Floor • San Francisco, CA 94103–1741

SS91 **Serving Students with Disabilities**
Holley A. Belch
Explores the critical role that community and dignity play in creating a meaningful educational experience for students with disabilities and shows how to help these students gain meaningful access and full participation in campus activities. Addresses such common concerns as fulfilling legal requirements and overcoming architectural barriers, as well as effective approaches to recruitment and retention, strategies for career and academic advising, and the impact of financial resources on funding programs and services.
ISBN: 0-7879-5444-6

SS90 **Powerful Programming for Student Learning: Approaches That Make a Difference**
Debora L. Liddell, Jon P. Lund
Assists student affairs professionals as they plan, implement, and evaluate their educational interventions on college and university campuses. Details each step of program assessment, planning, implementation, and outcome evaluation. Explains the importance of collaborating with faculty and others, illustrating several types of programming partnerships with four brief case studies, and examines the significant partnership aspects that led to programming success.
ISBN: 0-7879-5443-8

SS89 **The Role Student Aid Plays in Enrollment Management**
Michael D. Coomes
Discusses the political and cultural contexts that influence decisions about student aid and enrollment management, the special enrollment management challenges facing independent colleges, and some alternative methods for financing a college education. Provides a review of the research on the impact of student aid on recruitment and retention, recommendations for ethical enrollment planning, and a list of resources for enrollment planners, researchers, and policymakers.
ISBN: 0-7879-5378-4

SS88 **Understanding and Applying Cognitive Development Theory**
Patrick G. Love, Victoria L. Guthrie
Reviews five theories of the cognitive development of college students and explores the applications of those theories for student affairs practice. These theories shed light on gender-related patterns of knowing and reasoning; interpersonal, cultural, and emotional influences on cognitive development; and people's methods of approaching complex issues and defending what they believe.
ISBN: 0-7879-4870-5

SS87 **Creating Successful Partnerships Between Academic and Student Affairs**
John H. Schuh, Elizabeth J. Whitt
Presents case studies of academic and student affairs partnerships that have been successfully put into practice at a variety of institutions, in areas such as service learning, the core curriculum, and residential learning communities.
ISBN: 0-7879-4869-1

SS86   **Beyond Borders: How International Developments Are Changing**
International Affairs Practice
Diane L. Cooper, James M. Lancaster
Assesses the impact of international trends and developments on the student
affairs profession, and offers practical suggestions for developing the
knowledge and skills requisite for a global future. Explains how to recruit
and support international students and provide valuable information on
student and staff exchange programs. Presents case studies from student
affairs professionals in Mexico, Germany, and Hong Kong, highlighting the
global student affairs issues that transcend national borders.
ISBN: 0-7879-4868-3

SS85   **Student Affairs Research, Evaluation, and Assessment: Structure and**
Practice in an Era of Change
Gary D. Malaney
Describes how student affairs and faculty can collaborate to create an agenda
for student-related research; review technological aids for collecting and
analyzing data; and discusses how student affairs researchers can make their
role more vital to the campus by expanding into policy analysis and
information brokering.
ISBN: 0-7879-4216-2

SS84   **Strategies for Staff Development: Personal and Professional Education in**
the 21st Century
William A. Bryan, Robert A. Schwartz
Offers a range of strategies for recruiting, retaining, and developing an
educated, energetic, and motivated student affairs staff. Examines a
performance-based approach to human resource development, the impact of
supervisors and mentors on those entering and advancing in the field, and
the influence of behavioral style on professional development.
ISBN: 0-7879-4455-6

SS83   **Responding to the New Affirmative Action Climate**
Donald D. Gehring
Explores how to achieve an economically, ethnically, spiritually, and
culturally diverse student body while complying with confusing and
sometimes conflicting laws and judicial pronouncements. Clarifies the law as
it relates to affirmative action in admissions and financial aid; discusses
alternatives to race-based methods for achieving diversity; and reports on a
national study of student affairs programs that have successfully used
affirmative action.
ISBN: 0-7879-4215-4

SS82   **Beyond Law and Policy: Reaffirming the Role of Student Affairs**
Diane L. Cooper, James M. Lancaster
Examines higher education's apparent over-reliance on policy and shows
how we can redirect our attention to the ethical and developmental issues
that underlie the undergraduate experience. Discusses how learning
communities and creeds can help achieve balance between policy and
personal responsibility; how to deal with student misconduct in a way that
both reduces the risk of litigation and furthers student development; and
how to promote multiculturalism without compromising individual rights
and freedoms.
ISBN: 0-7879-4214-6

United States Postal Service

Statement of Ownership, Management, and Circulation

1. Publication Title New Directions for Student Services	2. Publication Number 0 1 6 4 - 7 9 7 0	3. Filing Date 9/28/01
4. Issue Frequency Quarterly	5. Number of Issues Published Annually 4	6. Annual Subscription Price $65 - Individual $130 - Institutio

7. Complete Mailing Address of Known Office of Publication (Not printer) (Street, city, county, state, and ZIP+4)
989 Market St
San Francisco, CA 94103
(San Franciso County)

Contact Person Joe Schuman
Telephone 415-782-3232

8. Complete Mailing Address of Headquarters or General Business Office of Publisher (Not printer)

Same as Above

9. Full Names and Complete Mailing Addresses of Publisher, Editor, and Managing Editor (Do not leave blank)

Publisher (Name and complete mailing address)
Jossey-Bass, A Wiley Company
(Above Address)

Editor (Name and complete mailing address) John H. Schuh
N243 Lagomarcino Hall
Iowa State University
Ames, IA 50011

Managing Editor (Name and complete mailing address)
None

10. Owner (Do not leave blank. If the publication is owned by a corporation, give the name and address of the corporation immediately followed by the names and addresses of all stockholders owning or holding 1 percent or more of the total amount of stock. If not owned by a corporation, give the names and addresses of the individual owners. If owned by a partnership or other unincorporated firm, give its name and address as well as those of each individual owner. If the publication is published by a nonprofit organization, give its name and address.)

Full Name	Complete Mailing Address
John Wiley & Sons Inc.	605 Third Avenue New York, NY 10158-0012

11. Known Bondholders, Mortgagees, and Other Security Holders Owning or Holding 1 Percent or More of Total Amount of Bonds, Mortgages, or Other Securities. If none, check box ▶ ☐ None

Full Name	Complete Mailing Address
Same As Above	Same as Above

12. Tax Status (For completion by nonprofit organizations authorized to mail at nonprofit rates) (Check one)
The purpose, function, and nonprofit status of this organization and the exempt status for federal income tax purposes:
☐ Has Not Changed During Preceding 12 Months
☐ Has Changed During Preceding 12 Months (Publisher must submit explanation of change with this statement)

PS Form 3526, October 1999   (See Instructions on Reverse)

---

13. Publication Title New Directions for Student Services	14. Issue Date for Circulation Data Below Summer 2001	
15. Extent and Nature of Circulation	Average No. Copies Each Issue During Preceding 12 Months	No. Copies of Single Issue Published Nearest to Filing Date

			Average	Single
a. Total Number of Copies (Net press run)			1,997	1,627
b. Paid and/or Requested Circulation	(1)	Paid/Requested Outside-County Mail Subscriptions Stated on Form 3541. (Include advertiser's proof and exchange copies)	729	719
	(2)	Paid In-County Subscriptions Stated on Form 3541 (Include advertiser's proof and exchange copies)	0	0
	(3)	Sales Through Dealers and Carriers, Street Vendors, Counter Sales, and Other Non-USPS Paid Distribution	0	0
	(4)	Other Classes Mailed Through the USPS	0	0
c. Total Paid and/or Requested Circulation [Sum of 15b. (1), (2),(3),and (4)] ▶			729	719
d. Free Distribution by Mail (Samples, complimentary, and other free)	(1)	Outside-County as Stated on Form 3541	0	0
	(2)	In-County as Stated on Form 3541	0	0
	(3)	Other Classes Mailed Through the USPS	1	1
e. Free Distribution Outside the Mail (Carriers or other means)			103	103
f. Total Free Distribution (Sum of 15d. and 15e.) ▶			104	104
g. Total Distribution (Sum of 15c. and 15f) ▶			833	823
h. Copies not Distributed			1,164	804
i. Total (Sum of 15g. and h.) ▶			1,997	1,627
j. Percent Paid and/or Requested Circulation (15c. divided by 15g. times 100)			88%	87%

16. Publication of Statement of Ownership
☒ Publication required. Will be printed in the Winter 2001 issue of this publication.   ☐ Publication not required.

17. Signature and Title of Editor, Publisher, Business Manager, or Owner Susan E Lewis
Vice President & Publisher - Periodicals
Date 9/28/01

I certify that all information furnished on this form is true and complete. I understand that anyone who furnishes false or misleading information on this form or who omits material or information requested on the form may be subject to criminal sanctions (including fines and imprisonment) and/or civil sanctions (including civil penalties).

Instructions to Publishers

1. Complete and file one copy of this form with your postmaster annually on or before October 1. Keep a copy of the completed form for your records.

2. In cases where the stockholder or security holder is a trustee, include in items 10 and 11 the name of the person or corporation for whom the trustee is acting. Also include the names and addresses of individuals who are stockholders who own or hold 1 percent or more of the total amount of bonds, mortgages, or other securities of the publishing corporation. In item 11, if none, check the box. Use blank sheets if more space is required.

3. Be sure to furnish all circulation information called for in item 15. Free circulation must be shown in items 15d, e, and f.

4. Item 15h., Copies not Distributed, must include (1) newsstand copies originally stated on Form 3541, and returned to the publisher, (2) estimated returns from news agents, and (3), copies for office use, leftovers, spoiled, and all other copies not distributed.

5. If the publication had Periodicals authorization as a general or requester publication, this Statement of Ownership, Management, and Circulation must be published; it must be printed in any issue in October or, if the publication is not published during October, the first issue printed after October.

6. In item 16, indicate the date of the issue in which this Statement of Ownership will be published.

7. Item 17 must be signed.

Failure to file or publish a statement of ownership may lead to suspension of Periodicals authorization.

PS Form 3526, October 1999 (Reverse)